KARL BARTH

Prophet of a New Christianity

by

WILHELM PAUCK

*Professor of Church History and
Historical Theology at the Chicago
Theological Seminary*

WIPF & STOCK · Eugene, Oregon

Wipf and Stock Publishers
199 W 8th Ave, Suite 3
Eugene, OR 97401

Karl Barth
Prophet of a New Christianity
By Pauck, Wilhelm
Copyright©1931 by Pauck, Wilhelm
ISBN 13: 978-1-5326-4155-8
Publication date 9/29/2017
Previously published by Harper & Brothers Publishers, 1931

KARL BARTH

Prophet of a New
Christianity

FOREWORD TO THE 2018 EDITION

WILHELM PAUCK WAS 30 years old when he published his first book in the United States of America. Keenly aware that the thought of Karl Barth had been neglected in this country, he introduced Barth and his thought in a unique way. In the first half of the book, Pauck describes the basic principles of Barth's theology, seeming to be in agreement with his point of view; in the second part of the book, however, Pauck is audaciously critical of the great theologian's ideas. Any thoughtful reader must come to his own conclusion.

The ensuing correspondence between Barth and Pauck, as yet unpublished, represents a brilliant and lively debate that continued through their lifetime. Pauck sent a signed copy of his book to Barth shortly after publication. A few months later, on Christmas Eve of 1931, Barth dictated a three page, single-spaced typed letter to the young author, protesting some of the criticism, but admitting that he was less annoyed since he had discovered that Pauck was German and had studied with Harnack, Holl, and Troeltsch at the University of Berlin. A second, milder exchange occurred in March and June of 1932. Barth suggested that Pauck might be better off discussing Tillich's ideas. Indeed, Pauck became close friends of Tillich, and he and I joined forces in writing the first volume of our biography of that fascinating and brilliant philosopher-theologian nearly 50 years later.

Pauck and Barth each had a superb sense of humor that alleviated the tension of their disagreement. Barth even welcomed the photograph of himself that Pauck had sent to him, and obliged him with a signed photograph of his own. This photograph was always to be found on the wall of Pauck's study along with photographs of Harnack, Holl, Troeltsch, and Tillich. Thus, the two protagonists became and remained friends despite their opposing views.

Incidentally, Eugene Exman, the distinguished head of the Religious Books Department at Harper & Bros., as it was known at that time, created the title, adding a question mark over Pauck's opposition (*Karl Barth: Prophet of a New Christianity?*) We have removed the question mark in this 2017 edition because Barth did indeed become the prophet of a new Christianity. I am grateful to Ted Lewis who urged me to publish this book. He made several creative suggestions regarding this new edition for which I am grateful. It is my hope that this book will be of interest to history and to twentieth-century theology buffs all over the world.

Marion Pauck, Literary Executor
Mountain View, California
January 2018

PREFACE

THE name of Karl Barth seems to stand for the beginning of a new era in theology. The entire Protestant world is attending to his religious thought. For more than ten years, theological literature has been filled with discussions of Barthianism. The number of its critics is not small, but its followers are constantly growing in power. The younger generation of German theologians are thoroughly oriented to the writings of Barth and his friends. Protestants of America and Great Britain show an increasing interest in the religious discussions of the European continent, and the translations and expositions of the Barthian theology, which have appeared in recent years, have not satisfied their demand for information about it. This book has been written in answer to this need. As an essay in understanding, it is submitted to all who are interested in Barth. An attempt has been made to interpret his theology against the background of the history of modern religious thought since Schleiermacher and in relation to the religious mood of the present day.

It is not for me to say whether I have succeeded in such an endeavor. I tell my readers, however, that even after the completion of this study, I am unable to declare myself either wholly for or against Barth. The inner struggle which has accompanied the writing of this book has not yet come to an end. The word "crisis" which is so closely connected with Barthian theology is of great personal significance to me and, I suppose, to many another member of the younger generation.

A list of Barth's publications is given in the Appendix. There, too, all footnote references have been gathered in order to facilitate the reading of the text itself, and in view of the fact that they will be of interest chiefly to those who wish to study Barth's work in its original context.

All quotations from Barth's writing, as presented in the text, are translated from the original German. Passages from Douglas Horton's translation of *Das Wort Gottes und die Theologie* (see particularly pp. 56, 81 ff.), have been used with the kind permission of Mr. Sidney A. Weston.

To my friend Douglas Horton, who has the honor of having introduced Barth to American readers, I am deeply indebted for the painstaking care with which he has read the manuscript.

W. PAUCK.

CONTENTS

ix

KARL BARTH

Prophet of a New
Christianity

I

THE PROBLEMS OF THE MODERN CHURCH

MODERN Protestantism is activity itself. It continues its work in missions, steadily changing its methods
to adjust itself to new conditions at home and abroad.
It busies itself in the field of social ethics, keeping an
attentive eye upon all changes in modern society. It
develops various techniques in religious education. The
aggressive, adaptive Protestant mind continues the
plowing and tilling of all its fields.

But are these activities of the church grounded in
a clear impulse and are they directed by a definite vision
of a goal? Do the missionary bodies still know for
what purpose they are engaged in missions? They say
that their policy is one of sharing partnership. Some-
times they admit that they can no longer go among
the "heathen" as ambassadors of the truth. Not only
the unchristian aspects of Western civilization in general and the criticism that the Orientals raise against
it have shattered their confidence in themselves; they
admit that their message is undergoing radical changes,
and they do not know how to preach a changing gospel. Missionary leaders are often prone to say, "We
are religiously perplexed, but we continue to believe in
Christ and particularly in his gospel of love." Who

3

this Christ is and of what kind his love, is, however, not clearly stated.

The social activities of the churches render a similar impression. In ever new waves propaganda movements arise, proclaiming moral codes for social behaviour, defending some sort of morality in international, interracial, industrial and political relationships. Again and again ministers and laymen express deep concern for the problems of the family, of marriage, and of sexual life in general. They show a sincere interest for the difficult conflicts between urban and rural areas. They have even studied the problem of providing city people with milk and advised procedures looking to social justice. But the question where religion comes in is often forgotten.

Why should the church be responsible for all this? Is it an institution of social reform? If so, how must it be compared with other organizations erected for that particular purpose? What is distinctly religious and especially Christian in the remarkable reform-activities of the modern church? The answers to these and similar questions are indistinct. They generally avoid the issue by affirming that the church of Christ certainly ought to be a guide and educator toward true and good living.

And at once social ethics becomes the concern of the pedagogue. It is religious education that must furnish salvation. Consequently all classes and groups of society are being studied with the help of the methods of the modern sciences of psychology and sociology. Most complicated "techniques" of educational approach are being developed. Sunday-schools are being slowly reorganized and transformed, as trained teachers appear on the scene. But where is the confidence in

a distinctive, clearly defined task? Where is that religion that is to be taught? Where is it?

Visit a modern theological seminary! Speak to the
teachers! Interview the students! They will confess
to be interested in religion, particularly in its historical
and contemporary expressions and in its application.
The oftener you hear the magic word "religion" the
more puzzling it becomes. Very few indeed are able
to agree as to its meaning. There is no longer authority
about it. Religious thinking is a personal, private af-
fair, and some more or less skillful persons do their
thinking in public. Everyone carves out for himself
what he deems his religion. No wonder that the missionary impetus is shattered, that the social activity of
the church loses more and more of its distinctly
churchly character, that religious educators concern
themselves more with methods than with the substance
that is to be transmitted to the pupils!

But are there no theologians, men who will guard
and guide the thought of the church? Are there no
preachers who can speak with authority? Yes, there
are theologians and there are preachers, but their teachings are not inspired by certainty. The sincerest among
them prefer to be "seekers." Happy are those who with
the help of creeds furnished by the past can take a firm
position and review things from a fixed, objective,
seemingly absolute viewpoint! To be sure, they are still
numerous, and their attitude, sustained by thousands
of certainly sincere people, is impressive. But may one
not rightly ask whether their apparent confidence is
more inspired by the necessity of self-defense than by
certitude of conviction?

What has happened? If this sketch of the modern
"Christian mind" is true to the facts, what has oc-

curred to bring it into being? The answer is not far
to seek: We are told that we live in a new world, that
we belong to a generation that is witnessing fundamental transformations of human life. The industrial
period of western civilization has reached its climax.
The machine has finally affected every phase of living.
If we desire to live sincerely, if our ethics shall correspond to the world as it actually is, we can no longer
hold to philosophies of life which are not made for a
machine age.

Such ideas furnish the practical, concrete background for the endless discussions of the place of science in modern life. For, so all of us believe, science
has produced the myriad technical facilities in private
and public life which are characteristic of our era. It
has accelerated the tempo of living. It has increased
the effectiveness of our actions. It has assured man of
a place in the life of the universe of which his ancestors
not even dreamed. It has made human life universal.
We find ourselves, therefore, compelled to accept practical methods of living which do not always correspond to the beliefs and philosophies which we hold.

Since what we actually do is of a more direct concern to us than what we think, we acquire the modern
way of living and postpone the development of a basic,
organizing thought until a later, more opportune time.
Most of us wait for *the* prophet and for *the* philosopher
who can tell us what we ought to think and to believe.
That is why we as Christians confess religious perplexity while continuing to believe in Christ.

Many of us are aware of this tentativeness of our
beliefs. This is the crisis of religion. For a religion
cannot be tentative. When the crisis has reached its
climax, its turning point, it will be known whether the

Christian church shall die or live. Some think the crisis is now at its peak. The present dispute over Theism and Humanism seems to prove it. It puts the question to us all: Do you believe in God or do you not? If we deny the question, we should not continue to call ourselves Christian or to consider ourselves members of the church.

It can hardly be doubted that most modern men are aware of this dilemma. The time of decision has come or will come soon. It is in anticipation of this decision and in consciousness of lacking clear direction that the churches and their leaders are so restless.

Not infrequently the issue is darkened. This is due to the fact that life does not stop. Men do not notice the radical nature of the changes that take place around them. Life proceeds. The inheritance of the past lives on. Its institutions are taken for granted. The church continues. People worship as their parents of old. Ministers continue to preach. Rites and customs are only very gradually changed. The decisiveness of a transformation is not felt. But a certain uneasiness is noticeable. There are churches where the scripture is only occasionally referred to and seldom preached about—as in days gone by. Many a church service presents in itself a striking contrast between a "modern" sermon which reviews various aspects of life from a moral and so-called religious viewpoint and an "ancient" liturgy and "old" music. But only few persons feel the contrast. The majority of church-goers feed their souls with the tunes of medieval chants and old Protestant chorals, and their intellects with the critical analyses offered by the more or less cultured minister in his discourse called the sermon. A historical institution may radically change, but the actual process of change is very gradual, and only after final results have been produced, do the adherents of such an institution become aware of it.

This general historical observation must be kept in mind in dealing with the transformation of the Christian world-view. The fundamental changes which so directly concern us emerged only step by step. That makes our situation only more difficult. Since, in order to live intelligently, we must cultivate our historical connections, we are hardly ever capable of judging our position in an objective way—from without, so to speak. To be sure, a few may make themselves believe that they can disregard the historical links of their intellectual life and construct philosophies on the basis of the present needs and with the help of those norms and laws which the present status of scientific understanding can lend them. And thus many a philosophy of religion is taught and preached. But the historically trained mind will only too easily recognize the connections also in this seemingly realistic, self-confident thought.

American Christianity is still, historically speaking, inarticulate. A history of its thought has not yet been written. Two facts, however, are outstanding. In the first place, American theology has been confined almost exclusively to denominational channels. Up to this day a large quantity of religious literature is put out for the benefit of denominationally limited groups. The thought-patterns of certain ecclesiastical traditions are reproduced or reinterpreted. The movements in the scientific and social-political world are reviewed from more or less fixed standpoints. Only more recently has American theology assumed a universal character. But at the same time it has often lost its definiteness, for the former relationship with a denominational heritage is replaced by an adjustment to a somewhat vague world of science and philosophy. The theological controversy between Modernism and Fundamentalism must be judged on the basis of the liberation of theological thought from ecclesiastical (denominational) authority. It is also not without significance that the propaganda for church union and interdenominationalism began at about the same time that theologians were breaking the chains of intellectual confinement to their denominational creeds. Modernization of religious thought and interdenominationalism go hand in hand. Only those denominational groups which never depended upon creeds or theological definitions, notably the Congregationalists, have been, throughout their history, liberal in their religious teachings.

The second outstanding phenomenon in the history of American Christianity is its gradual estrangement from Calvinism. It is still generally maintained that Calvinism is to the present day influential in American social life. But it cannot be doubted that the distinctly otherworldly, theocentric *religion* of three hundred years ago has today been replaced by a world-wide, anthropocentric religiousness. When the history of American theology is written, it will reveal an amazing story of the steady humanization of religious beliefs. Humanism is a logical result of tendencies which have long been active in American life. The two factors which have brought about this effect one will then probably discover to be Methodism and the Enlightenment.[1] It is important to note that these movements, of distinctly European origin, were to reach the peak of their influence on American soil. *Methodism* has certainly celebrated its greatest triumph in the conquest of the American West. Many of us are too little conscious of the debt that we owe to Methodism for the fashion in which we conduct our church-services: the majority of the Protestant hymns and sermons are Methodist-inspired. But surely the newspapers are aware of the significance of Wesley's church in social life and its reform! The *Enlightenment* has achieved its victories on the American continent in the political and scientific fields. The American constitution itself is a product of the "Age of Reason"; and the political and social ideals of America, which it has determined and which center around "the rights of man" and "democracy," bear the stamp of the eighteenth century which shattered the authorities of the past. Methodism has humanized religion by destroying the otherworldly, predestinarian, theocentric character of Calvinism. The Enlightenment gave to America not only the instrument of nature-control in which the whole world shares, but also the confidence in progress and the optimistic belief in the perfectibility of human life. The criticism of the Bible and of the Christian past constitutes only one phase in the process of the general humanization of religion. Only when the Enlightenment proclaimed the autonomy of man in contrast to any heteronomous authority, could the movements of historical criticism and of free investigation begin. When the Humanists of today profess their sole interest in the furthering of human happiness with complete disregard of any form of traditional authority, when the frankest among them declare the God of the Christian past dead, when they recognize in the God-idea only the symbolization of human ideals and hopes, they are true children of a development which has long been going on in America—and in the world. For centuries, religious thought has moved away from the idea of an otherworldly God. Religion has gradually become God-less. Whether there can be a religion without God, a godless religion, is the question which constitutes the present crisis of religion. The answer to this question will determine the future of the Christian church. In other words, we must decide whether we are to stay within the channel of the historical development of Christianity since the Enlightenment or whether we can leave it in the conviction that our recent ancestors were obsessed by a serious error in judgment. Whether man is God—that is the question. When we say yes, we have ceased to be Christians in the old sense of the word.

Such is the condition of Christian theology in America. It is not fundamentally different in other countries except that the trends of different pasts, as they affect the present situation, have resulted in varying emphases. It is especially interesting to study conditions in Germany,[2] which since the days of the Reformation, and especially since Schleiermacher, has produced the most influential of the theological systems.

German theology has held a peculiar place in public life. Unlike the usual American practice the theological faculties have always been members of the universities. They have been engaged in their research under full loyalty to the scientific principles of investigation as these are generally observed in the institutions of higher learning. This loyalty and freedom accounts for the advances made by German Protestant theology. Conflicts between the theological faculties and the churches and their authorities have been numerous. For German Protestantism with its Lutheran and partly Calvinistic background is distinctly confessional. The professors of theology did not always promote the interests of the ecclesiastical group to which they nominally belonged. The majority of them, of course, knew and know well how to combine the academic-theological with the practical-ecclesiastical points of view without doing harm to or hampering either one. It is, however, not without interest to note that Harnack, a man of highest theological importance, never held an ecclesiastical position, because he fell temporarily in disgrace with the ecclesiastical bureaucrats, being accused of endangering the piety of the church by his historical research. The history of theology in Germany has therefore not been without practical complications, but it has derived its distinction from an interrelationship between academic research and practical church life.

Generally speaking, German theology is the most academic of all. It has become extraordinarily learned, both in its critical-historical and constructive-philosophical aspects. For this reason it has always been most sensitive to the changes and movements in the scientific and philosophical fields.

German theologians were strengthened in this attitude, because it was never practically contrary to the actual needs of the church. Although it is wrong to say that until recently the German Protestant Church had no social conscience and that its work was seldom generally social, being more concerned with the care of souls as a pastoral task, the general feeling expressed in such an opinion is true to the facts. The State fulfilled not only the financial but also many of the social duties which in countries where church and state are separated, fall to the church. The German Evangelical Church has been up to the present time chiefly a preaching church. The development and cultivation of church activities during recent years is remarkable, but the German minister is still primarily a theologian and a preacher. His training in the free, unprejudiced atmosphere of a university is therefore exceedingly adequate for his task. Only recently has the discussion about the relationship between church and university faculties become livelier. There is a certain irony in the fact that while American theological seminaries, usually tied to their churches, seek affiliation with universities, German theologians who for centuries have been active and honored members of the *universitas literarum* should now be discussing the possibility of the foundation of independent institutions of theological training.

All this helps us to understand why since the beginning of the last century distinguished generations of theological scholars have succeeded each other in Germany. As soon as modern critical thought was born, as soon as the modern sciences and philosophies unfolded their power (thanks to the effects of the Enlightenment), theology began its work of adaptation. The science of the Christian religion was in no way to stand behind the other fields of knowledge.

Just as in the case of America, Christian thought of Germany is profoundly affected by the "Illumination." Without awareness of this historical connection it is impossible to understand the German religion and theology of the present day. That the Enlightenment should hold such a place in the public life of our era is not surprising, for it was Germany which adopted its principles to their full extent. That movement which took its start in English Deism, being then transplanted into France, thereby becoming a vehicle of anti-religious and atheistic propaganda, was enlarged to a new system of philosophy when it reached Germany. German Idealism is said to have overcome the shortcomings of the Enlightenment, its rationalism and its moralism, but in reality it fulfilled it. To be sure, the philosophical speculations of the German Idealists cannot be fully understood without reference to the Lutheran reformation, but on the whole they are contrary to the spirit of the Christian religion. Modern philosophy as it was inaugurated by Descartes, establishing the autonomy of man as a rational being, reached its height in the thought of Kant, Fichte, and Hegel.

This development had a twofold effect upon the nineteenth century.

The Enlightenment successfully estranged the educated middle classes from orthodox and ecclesiastical Christianity. The effects of this emancipation became particularly evident in the foundation of secondary schools which in their instruction put the emphasis upon a humanistic education on the basis of the study of the ancient classics. The German "Gymnasium" is a product of the Enlightenment. Since the beginning of the last century it has become a stronghold of German Idealism. In accepting its world-view the educated German showed himself to have outlived the necessity of submitting to the religious authority of the church, particularly since in the classical poetry of Lessing, Schiller and Goethe he received the vision of a new, entirely satisfactory conception of life which charged him to pursue the ideal of a free, autonomous "personality" responsible only to the norms of the spirit within. The German middle classes thus became estranged from the church, and to this day it has not succeeded in winning them back. All these facts cast a significant light upon the current discussions of the relationship between Christianity and Idealism.

Practically speaking the Enlightenment achieved a glorious victory, which was to assume pathetically tragic aspects when, in the middle of the last century, Labor, led by leaders who had received their philosophies from the Idealists, was to follow the educated classes in emancipating itself from the church. But while the "cultured" maintained an attitude of indifference or benevolent neutrality toward organized religion, the people under the banner of socialism became more and more anti-Christian and "atheistic," venting all their class hatred upon the church. Of course, one cannot make the Enlightenment or Idealism responsible for this development, but that they stand in a certain connection with it cannot be doubted.

Meanwhile the church or at least its theological leaders were not blind to the changes that were taking place in the world of thought. It is true, German Protestantism did not realize the significance of the industrial revolution early enough to show direct concern for the new working classes and their problems. Its union with a patriarchal State was of catastrophic significance. However, it adopted the new worldview as outlined by the natural and historical sciences and by a critical philosophy. As a matter of fact, German theology was first in recognizing the new thought when it accepted the principles of Kant's philosophy. His claim that human knowledge can contain only the sensate experiences as they are classified by the *a priori* forms and categories of the mind and his proof that all possibility of a knowledge of the

supernatural must be excluded from the realm of reason, were to become fundamental principles of "modern" theology. Kant's own theological thought was
not accepted; it was too moralistic. The God-idea was
to him nothing but a postulate which had to be made
in order to guarantee the laws of "practical reason."
Due to his work, however, autonomous thinking was
definitely established in theology, and the distinction
between world knowledge and religious knowledge became a common premise of the advanced theologians.
This distinction was to be of the most fatal consequences; for German theology derived therefrom the
right not to concern itself seriously with the natural
sciences. When the error had to be corrected, it was
too late.

Furthermore, Kant's claim that the object of knowledge, the *Ding an sich* must remain unapproachable
and unknowable and that objects of faith in particular
can never become objects of knowledge at all, forced
theology to pay attention to the subject of faith.
Schleiermacher, by placing religion in the realm of feeling and by defining theology as the description of
pious feelings, inaugurated the period of psychologism.
The psychological method was followed in all endeav-
ors to understand the religious phenomenon. Ritschl,
imbued with Kantian and positivistic philosophical
principles, tried to avoid the pit of subjectivism by
emphasizing the importance of history for the Christian religion. The Christian God-idea was not guaranteed by personal experience but by the historical Jesus.

Psychologism dissolves all possibility of a proof of
absolute religious truth. Religion depends wholly
upon personal religious experience and is limited to the
experiencing individual. Neither can historism, logi-

cally thought out, give the assurance of an objective fact or truth, but leads inevitably to a relativism, which can admit the existence of an absolute only in so far as it expresses itself in the limitation of a historical fact.

Under these influences a more complete and thorough analysis of the religious life was made possible, but its objective validity became questionable. The God-idea especially was appreciated as a function within the human mind rather than as a recognition of the reality of the existence of God.

The organized church more or less instinctively felt the danger involved. The new theology seemed to contradict the traditions which were kept alive in its midst. But the spirit of the Enlightenment gradually produced an individualism within the church which could no longer be reconciled with any form of objective or absolute authority. Thus the problem of revelation became paramount. The future of Christianity in its traditional form hinged upon the problem whether its revelation was objective or not. If the premises of modern theology were correct, it could be but a certain phase or attitude of the human mind.

The point of a decision was reached: Either traditional Christianity or modern theology was right. The two could not be reconciled with each other, in spite of the fact that in the use of theological terminology, one was attempting a practical compromise.

Such was the dilemma in German theological thought in consequence of the Enlightenment and the critical Idealism of Kant at the beginning of the twentieth century. Only the end of the Great War revealed its all-important implications. The practical significance of a seemingly academic issue was then made apparent.

The full rise of Neo-Protestantism occurred in the period of the development of the German Empire after the Franco-Prussian War of 1870–71. The era of empire-building was a time of general progress and of the unfolding power of self-confidence. The findings of all the sciences, theology included, seemed to coincide with the upward trend of a new historical epoch. The imperial slogan: "I lead you into glorious times," apparently expressed a general sentiment. Warning voices were not heard. Nietzsche, with his gospel of the superman and the revaluation of all values, furnished the world-view of the times. His pathetic attempt to renew the foundations of a breaking civilization, and the underlying pessimism with which his philosophy was imbued were not recognized in their true nature. In reality the period was one of shallow, self-sufficient materialism, in spite of its evident progress in the accumulation of cultural values. Its true nature came to light with the outbreak of the war. The terror of that experience led to a general disillusionment. Cultural optimism was replaced by the shadows of a sceptical pessimism.

The author of the "Decline of the West" voiced the feeling of all. In feverish enthusiasm thousands of hungry souls read the heavily-laden pages of an unusual historical book in order to have the trend of their times analyzed in the light of world history.

The youth movement, which had sprung up as a revolt of young people against the civilization of the big cities and which had developed into a rebellion against the authority of the elders of school, church and home, seemed justified. The glorious progress into a better world was halted. How terrifying the awakening really was in the midst of post-war conditions, revolutions, famines, foreign oppression, inflations and a general breakdown of the economic order, is a story which is still to be written. For the German adult and for the German youth in particular there was only one attitude to take: Mistrust the world as it is and the power which permeates it—express your own self. The magic of the romanticism of self-expression could furnish the only salvation. Expressionism in literature and art; mysticism and the occult exercises of Theosophy and Anthroposophy in religion; communistic, socialistic, democratic ideologies in politics; abandonment of the old rules of sexual relationship and married life—all these reveal the age of disillusionment, when man returned from the world, which he thought he could conquer, to his own self, seeking hope and relief in the seemingly unbounded dreams of his soul.

Yet this life was not a revival, it did not bring relief. It was rather the expression of despair. It supposedly provided an escape from a destroyed world and from a cultural turmoil. Actually men merely retreated from their wider, secular selves into the secret chambers of the soul and its hidden, partly unspeakable longings. The world they had built was in upheaval and ruin: where else could they go—but to themselves!

This was the last, most pathetic, most tragic phase of a period of civilization which in amazing feats of progress had tried to prove that man was to rule the world and that it was his. At the end—man was alone.

But in solitariness is also the hope for a new beginning. In solitariness is hell and heaven. It furnishes despair and respite. It is a crisis, and a crisis is a turn-ing point.

And German man began his recovery. The first signs of his convalescence soon became apparent. The painters ceased to fill the art-galleries with the unproportioned, wildly-colored products of a fever-ish, frantic imagination; the contours of the world as we see it returned and the laws of perspective were no longer violently disobeyed. The subjectivism of their revolutionary art was replaced by what they called a "new objectivism," a "new realism." Soon after-wards the architects inaugurated a new building period by erecting structures of a restrained purposefulness, combining comfort and practical adequacy with simple beauty. The philosophers followed. Phenom-enology attempts to overcome the conflicts between objectivism and subjectivism. It aims at a meaningful realism. Nor do other kinds of human endeavor lag far behind. In every field, there is the beginning of a plan of reconstruction, which observe new laws and rules, described in terms like concreteness, objectivism, factualism, *Sachlichkeit.*

Ideologies and Utopias are shattered. One must reckon with the facts of life as they actually are. The fever has not yet stopped. The crisis is not yet passed. There is still sickness, but there is new hope of life. An upward trend has begun.

Naturally, religion was to suffer most, for man is most sensitive in his religious consciousness. The proc-ess of recuperation is here therefore slowest—but here too it is going on. A new theology is in the making.

What is this new theology? Is it connected with the name of Karl Barth, whose books are spoken of all over the world? Is it the so-called theology of crisis?

Some answer this question with a violent negative, others with a most enthusiastic affirmative.

In the next chapters this theology will be discussed at length. The results of the discussion will reveal our answer. They will disclose whether Barth is the prophet of a new Christianity or whether we must wait for another.

II

THE THEOLOGICAL BACKGROUND OF BARTHIANISM

It may be well to state the general character of Barth's theology in the light of the previous chapter, before a detailed discussion of his work is undertaken.

The first important characteristic of Barthianism that must be stressed is that Barth and his followers claim to stand outside of orthodoxy and fundamentalism as well as beyond modernism. Such an attitude deserves our full attention. Everyone who has made the problems of the church his own feels that the discussion about the place of liberalism in modern Christianity belongs to yesterday. No intelligent person will deny the validity of the demand that the church recognize the modern world-view as it has been shaped by the results of scientific research. A defense of the story of the creation as it is told in the first chapters of the Bible against the theory of evolution is an act of blind stubbornness. A denial of the human origin of the Bible and a refusal to investigate the history of the Church according to the best scholarly methods is dishonest. To retain a theology of yesterday, which does not do justice to modern astronomy, geology, biology and psychology, is impossible. But there can be no doubt about the fact that some of the critics of the Church have allowed the modern world to crowd out not only antiquated theological and ecclesiastical customs and views, but the essence of Christianity itself. Whenever the movement of modernism assumes such radical proportions, the Church, in so far as it is made up of people who sincerely cling to its faith, must rise against it and shake it off. For such a proceeding it can find many an example in its past.

Because some of the critics of the Church have gone out of bounds, fundamentalism and orthodoxy feel newly justified. They can at least claim to have kept the faith and to have been loyal to the religious content of the Christian gospel. It is for this reason that hosts of people and particularly a growing number of younger men and women are attracted to it. For they feel that it is after all better to have a vital faith in outworn clothing and make-up than to be dressed in the most recent apparel, accredited by fashion, but have hardly any faith left. The slogan of the liberals that a Christian ought not refuse to be intelligent has had its good effect, but it really does not refer to the essential need. For do not most of us depend more upon the cry of the heart than upon the reasoning of the brain? While it is true that in our desire to live unified lives, we are inclined not to hold to forms of a religious faith which are in clear contrast to what our minds know, it is also a fact that there are only few who really attain that complete harmony. Most human beings have more than one soul.

This explains why perfectly intelligent men will believe in the literal inspiration of the Bible, in the resurrection of Lazarus, and even in the creation of the world as recorded in Gen. 1, and in the fall of Adam and Eve, as if all these things were unshakable facts. If the modern Church wants to be sincere, however, must it not discard these and similar convictions and hold to its faith in the revelation of God in Jesus Christ, which orthodox Christians so bravely and enthusiastically profess and for which many a person among them brings the *sacrificium intellectus?*

Obviously, therefore, many men today sympathize with both camps of modern theology which until recently were hostile. These men will notice with great interest that Barthianism fights against two fronts, against liberalism *and* against orthodoxy, that it agrees with the most radical schools of Biblical criticism, while it professes to be attracted by the dogma of the inspired Bible.

The question how such an attitude can be taken leads us to the second significant characteristic of the theology of Barth. He opposes both modernism and fundamentalism while recognizing elements of worth in them both, on the basis of the teaching that God has revealed himself in the word, and that this teaching with all its implications constitutes the true Christian faith. In other words: Barth presents certain doctrines of God, the word, and the revelation which he declares must be accepted or at least developed if modern Christianity is to extricate itself from the dilemma into which it is placed by the struggle between tradition and the demands of the modern era.

The most important of the doctrines just mentioned is that of revelation. It presents the central problem in the religious thought of our day. If it could be shown that such a doctrine must still be held and how it could be accepted, the Christian church would be filled with new life. Modern discussion on the truth of Christianity hinges namely on the claim that the true knowledge of God which is identical with the revelation of him is obtainable in Jesus Christ. The modernists have destroyed this belief by depriving it of its absoluteness; orthodox Christians still hold on to it with the help of an inadequate philosophy.

By calling attention to the doctrine of revelation, we have pointed to the most vital concern of Barth. Only those who put the emphasis upon this aspect of his theology truly understand him and the extraordinary place which has been allotted to him in the theological world.

It will therefore be of value briefly to review the present state of the discussion of the problem of revelation and its historical background. We shall then be prepared to analyze Barth's teachings in detail.

Revelation as an *idea* is as old as religion, as old as men's reverent attention to something in life which does not seem to originate from facts or inherently belong to them as their own product. Rather, revelation seems to transcend facts and descend upon them from a "Yonder."

Revelation[1] as a religious-philosophical *concept*, and thus used in Christian theology, is the product of oriental-semitic apocalypticism and of hellenistic philosophy. In its first aspect, it is the revelation (the disclosure) of a divine plan for the world. The bearer of the revelation is the seer who has been privileged to behold transcendent mysteries. In its second aspect, it is the result of a need of later Greek philosophy, a need for a faith which should be exempt from the uncertainties of philosophical discussions. Greek philosophy, in its attempt to understand and form life on the basis of theoretical reason, ended in scepticism. Instead of finding a meaning of life, it had to admit the inability of human reason to control life's content. In such a crisis there was introduced the concept of revelation, as it was contained in the religious traditions of the East.

Two elements, then, constitute the concept of revelation: The unveiling of a hidden, as yet unknown (coming) event and the disclosing of a hidden faith (which reason is unable to develop from itself). These two elements were united on Christian soil by the Apologists, the Christian writers of the second century: The revelation has taken place in Jesus Christ; in him the divine world-plan is fulfilled, and in him the truth has appeared for which the Greeks searched in vain.

As long as a supernaturalistic world-view remained in force, this concept of revelation was the basis of all Christian claims of possessing the divine truth. As such it is still retained by Catholicism and by certain orthodox protestant groups. At the Renaissance, however, reason began again to become autonomous. The work of the Greeks was renewed. The ecclesiastical tradition, particularly in Protestantism, had to yield to this development, and gradually surrendered its supernatural system of faith to the admission that there can be no other approach to the understanding of life and its facts but that of reason or such experiences which are controllable or explicable by reason. Thus Rationalism dissolved the orthodox concept of revelation.

The objections[2] against the belief in a revelation are chiefly three: The first objection is that all that is, stands in correlation. The total reality must be comprehended as the total correlation of all single things or beings. There are no isolated facts or events which cannot be related to this total reality. The historian, of course, will claim that with every human individuality something new appears in the total content of things, but each individuality is a relation and never an absolute fact. The Christian idea of a revelation of God in Christ cannot therefore be defended.

The second is that it is intolerable to modern thinking that one single historical phenomenon should contain the absolute truth. The world is infinite in its physical and spiritual character; it cannot have a center. The revelation of God in Jesus Christ seems to be the absolutization of a historical fact which is significant only to the Western world in its history of the last 1900 years.

And the third is that the modern world-view is characterized by its belief in the powers of reason. Reason is the measure and norm of all knowledge. Revelation as something that is not knowable by reason, either in the past or in the future, would be contrary to the claim that reason in its investigation of the facts and their content constitutes knowledge of truth.

It is seldom realized that these three elements upon which the modern world-view is founded, namely the belief in the relativity of all things; the belief, which follows from this, that one single or singularized fact cannot contain all or absolute truth; and the belief in the adequacy of reason for the establishment of truth, destroys religion as a faith in a God who is supernatural. That is, if these elements of the modern world-view are adequate for the discovery of the meaning of life, all supernatural revelation of the divine truth must be given up. Quite apart from all the problems which must be raised in regard to the person of Jesus Christ, the problem of the existence of God and the kind of existence in particular which he enjoys would be insoluble.

But, as a matter of fact, the rationalistic modern world-view is firmly entrenched only against supernaturalism, not against religion or belief in God as such. The religious experience of the presence of God who reveals himself in and to his believers is something that is exempt from the criticism of reason. It cannot be touched by it. Only if such a belief is coordinated with a supernaturalistic philosophy, when the being of God is identified with supernature, is its criticism valid.

The task of the modern Christian is therefore as of old to reconcile revelation and reason. Only if he should be able to develop an ontology which would allow him to speak of the existence, of the actuality of God, in terms that are not offensive to and not out of agreement with the irrefutable principles of the modern scientific world-view could he maintain a justifiable idea of revelation. In these discussions it should be remembered that religion is not identical with supernaturalism, which is a metaphysical theory, but that such a philosophy was introduced into the Christian thought when it began to become philosophical-theological. For centuries, the theory of supernaturalism proved sufficient for all purposes of philosophical justification of the religious belief in God. It explained how God could *be*.

It would be a wrong conclusion to say that with the breakdown of the supernaturalistic theory the belief in the reality of God also has to fall. The tragedy of such a conclusion, to be sure, has often occurred. But that it is unnecessary and avoidable is clearly evinced by the fact that people will not cease to be religious—*i.e.*, to believe in a God even if they have no philosophical argument for such a conviction. To dismiss the validity of this observation by saying that people are then stupidly loyal to a tradition, or that they are superstitious, shows a lack in the understanding of the nature of religion. For it must simply be admitted—and it can be proved by an analysis of the history and the psychology of religion—that religion is identical with having a God and that having a God is a human necessity, the "why" and "how" of which can be explained only inadequately. The very fact that the ages of so-called intellectual and religious scepticism happen to be the ages of most lively religious vitality and even fertility should give pause to those who think they possess reasons or grounds which would explain religion or even explain it away. History teaches that men will not stop believing in God when philosophies and theologies, yes, even religious institutions and churches—fail. The prophets who have foreseen the death of God seem to have been "misinformed." Those of their kind whom we now have among us, prophesying a future so glorious that it will not need God, have driven many of their pupils and followers into the dark and lowly halls where philosophically and otherwise disillusioned men are gathered in search of a revelation. The cults of Occultism, Mysticism, Spiritualism, Theosophy, Anthroposophy which spread in the cities of the western world as formerly they did in the Roman Empire disclose the pathetic fact that even religious sceptics will look and wait for a revelation of the divine. No man can live without a God. And the divine is never found by reasoning. It is just here. It reveals itself.

Revelation outlasts any theory devised to explain or

justify it, but man will not rest until he has replaced a bankrupt philosophy or theory by a new one.

When it became evident that supernaturalism could not withstand the growing power of Rationalism and that it would be superseded by new systems of thought, the theologians adjusted themselves to the new conditions. They let the metaphysics of supernaturalism go, hoping to retain the *fact* in which they believed and for the sake of which they philosophized, namely, revelation.

It remains now to consider the methods and results of this adjustment, for Barth considers it a faulty and erroneous one. He claims that the Christian thinkers of the last century set out on the wrong track, and that another new beginning must be made.

The problem under review is simply this: How did the theologians speak of the "being" of God if it could not be described in terms of supernature, if revelation could not be identified with supernaturalistic doctrine? The answer of *Schleiermacher* was decisive. He was well aware of the difficulty. He attempted to solve the problem on the basis of a clear analysis. Although he did not develop a definite doctrine of revelation, he paid attention to the place which it holds in the religious life. His famous paragraph on the definition of piety or religion as "the consciousness of being absolutely dependent, or, which is the same thing, of being in relation with God," contains the following sentence:[3] "If we speak of an original revelation of God to man or in man, the meaning will always be just this, that along with the absolute dependence which characterizes not only man but all temporal existence, there is given to man also the immediate self-consciousness of God." Religion is primarily a quality of life, a "feeling," the character of which in distinction from other feelings, is described by the term "consciousness of God." This term implies a definite understanding of the way in which God "*is*." Schleiermacher speaks of it in the following statement:[4] "Any possibility of God being in any way *given* is entirely excluded, because anything that *is* outwardly given must be given as an object exposed to our counter-influence, however slight this may be. The transference of the idea of God to any perceptible object, unless one is all the time conscious that it is a piece of purely arbitrary symbolism, is always a corruption, whether it be a temporary transference—*i.e.*, a theophany, or a constitutive transference, in which God is represented as permanently a particular perceptible existence." Schleiermacher deserves high credit for this remarkably lucid emphasis that God, in order to be God, can never be objectively given, as inanimate things or even conscious persons are given.

Here Schleiermacher, the "father of modern theology," shared the opinion of the idealistic philosophers. Shall we then suppose that he agreed with the Idealists in their ontological monism of the spirit, in their teaching that God is *immanent* in the human mind in so far as it comes to itself, becomes conscious? We shall be in a position to answer this question as we proceed to investigate how Schleiermacher defined God's "existence" or "way of being" positively, the statement that God is not "given" being only negative.

The question how God is, finds its answer in the concept of revelation, for it is in revelation that God discloses himself as he is. If we search then for Schleiermacher's definition of "revelation" we find the following statement:[5] ". . . the idea of revelation signifies the *originality* of the fact which lies at the foundation of a religious communion, in the sense that this fact, as conditioning the individual content of the religious emotions which are found in the communion, cannot itself in turn be explained by the historical chain which precedes it." This interpretation is in general harmony with Schleiermacher's concept of religion. It stresses the individuality and the positive character of piety. But as a matter of fact, it describes the formal character of *all* piety. It is natural to assume that Christianity is not exempt from this description. Its revelation must therefore be one among others. It does not seem to possess an exclusive, absolute character. Wherein is it, then, distinctive? Wherein lies the "originality" of its revelation? The answer Schleiermacher attempts is that "in it everything is related to the redemption accomplished by Jesus of Nazareth," who "is like all men in virtue of the ideality of human nature, but distinguished from them all by the constant potency of his God-consciousness, which was a veritable existence of God in him." [6] The positive character of the Christian revelation must be derived from Jesus Christ, and it is *his* God-consciousness that discloses to us how God is. This is, indeed, a remarkable discovery! The divine revelation is "neither an absolutely supernatural nor an absolutely supernational thing." The idea of revelation is "better applied only to the region of the higher self-consciousness." [7] Insofar as it is quickened in certain individuals, who are the heroes of religion and the founders of religious communions, it must be "inspired from the universal fountain of life."

We can now conclude that Schleiermacher, when he really defined the positive character of revelation, used an idealistic ontology. The "universal fountain of life," the universe, as he said in the "Addresses on Religion," finds expression in the higher self-consciousness. God is immanent in the human soul as it rises into perfect self-consciousness. This means that the absoluteness of the Christian revelation must be denied. Schleiermacher succeeded in establishing the positiveness and the individuality of all religions. They are original, more or less perfect, concretions and individualizations of the "infinite" that pervades the universe. In such manner he reconciled "modern" thought with the idea of revelation. It cannot be said, however, that he successfully retained the absolute character of the *Christian* idea of revelation, although he struggled for just that with all the power of his profoundly sensitive and marvelously facile mind. His work on "Christian faith" is the supreme expression of this struggle. He doubtless strove to present the belief of the Christian church, and the whole book is sincerely Christian in tone and intention. But his method, revolutionary as it was, did not permit him to say what ought to have been said. It was the method of introspection, of psychological self-analysis.[8] He was convinced that an investigation of the mode, of the "how" of religious apperception was the primary matter. He could never, therefore, make a positive statement about "God."

The theology of the nineteenth century lived on the heritage that Schleiermacher left. It confirmed the work of reconciliation between the beliefs of the Christian tradition and modern thought. It went beyond Schleiermacher chiefly in dealing with the problems of Christian revelation, which the "father of modern theology" had only touched. The outstanding contribution was that of *A. Ritschl* and his school. Their thought was based on an ontology inspired by Kant. Strictly opposed to any form of metaphysics, they transformed Kant's epistemological dualism of nature and mind into an ontological one. They distinguished between two ultimate elements which constitute the universe: the world of nature as a law-governed mechanism and the world of spiritual, moral personalities endowed with an ethical autonomy. The unity of these two worlds is established by God who as supremely autonomous, world-governing will, reigns over nature according to the purposes of spiritual morality. This will of God is revealed in Jesus Christ, particularly in so far as he discloses the invitation of God to every man, in spite of his sin, to participate in the divine work for the establishment of the supreme moral purpose of all existence: the establishment of the Kingdom of God. In other words, the meaning of the revelation is the informing of the moral purposes of man, particularly in respect to his spiritual control over nature. *W. Herrmann* added to all this the significant thought that Jesus Christ reveals God as the absolute moral will which overpowers man whenever he comes under the influence of Jesus and enables him to live the good life. Religion and ethics are one.

This general theological thought enabled the Ritschlians to overcome the conflict between modern thought and Christianity.

A strict dualism between nature and spirit permitted them to accept the modern world-view while they retained their belief in the absoluteness of the Christian revelation. They could even tolerate the radical criticism concerning the life of Jesus and accept the findings of New Testament research which relativized Jesus in every respect, and still maintain the conviction that his moral supremacy and its renewing power was *the* revelation of God.

If we ask what the Ritschlians have to contribute to our problem, how God is (if he is not supernature) we discover the following: They agree with Schleiermacher in the conviction that God cannot be objectively given. He is understood in connection with the ethical phase of life. Herrmann in particular never tires of stressing the point that God is supreme love, identical with regenerating forgiveness. The uniqueness of the Christian gospel is thus preserved and seemingly also the truth of the religious experience of revelation, namely its transcendent character. Life is fulfilled when it is controlled by the surrender to a love which cannot be attained by natural powers but must be disclosed in its otherness.

Two serious objections, however, must be raised against this view. In the first place, is not God limited to one sphere of existence, to the spiritual-ethical sphere? How is he related to the realm of nature? Must we not speak of the being, the qualitative existence of God in such a way that it will concern the whole of life and not only part of it? Ritschl felt the problem, but when he attempted a solution he came again close to supernaturalism in assuming a world-governing will which *uses* nature for the achievement of its purpose.

Curiously enough, current American humanism finds itself involved in the same dilemma. In some cases, it presents really Ritschlian ideas in an agnostic, atheistic make-up. It denies the presence of any moral teleology in nature. The universe is foreign to the spiritual ideals of man. When man pursues these ideals, he strives for the preservation of his human existence, hoping for the ultimate fulfillment of his dream of universal happiness of all mankind. The moral life is the expression of a natural endowment which man shares with all conscious beings, but which in him as the highest form of the evolution of life is best and most completely unfolded. One can well understand this philosophy of humanism as an agnostic form of Ritschlianism. Ritschl and his pupils were, so one may say, semi-agnostics, for their theological ontology did not comprehend the life of nature.

It is interesting to note the effect which Ritschlianism had upon some of its American followers. When they recognized the limitation of it in face of the modern American emphasis upon the place of science in life, they were unable to defend it. In consequence they became religious sceptics, refusing even to attempt the construction of a new ontology which would be in keeping with the concept of nature as science so convincingly presented it and do justice to the content of the Christian revelation, in the validity of which most of them still practically believed.

The second objection against the Ritschlian idea of revelation concerns Christology. It is maintained that in Jesus Christ the divine revelation of moral sublimity and love has found its ideal expression. Jesus Christ is *the* revealer, because the ethical ideal is in him absolutely realized. But this absoluteness is not really absolute. First of all, we have no right to confine the absolute to any relative phenomenon. Again, the Ritschlians and particularly Herrmann, never gave a clear answer to the question why the experience of divine revelation derives only from Jesus. It is said that he was the highest manifestation of the life of

God. But who judges whether he was the highest? Evidently the person who has the experience. Then there is no reason why someone should not claim to have experienced the manifestation of the divine in another than Jesus. Is this in accordance with the belief of the church that God revealed himself once for all in Jesus Christ? Evidently not! If this be true, should the church not give up its claim of possessing the absolute revelation?

It was Ernst *Troeltsch* who became the herald of those who felt they must confirm this conclusion. As a member of the religious-historical school of theology, he realized the impossibility of a historical isolation of Christianity, particularly as to its origin. Early Christianity appeared to be the result of the religious syncretism of the Graeco-Roman Empire. How could one then defend the opinion that the Christian church possessed *the* revelation? Naturally, the tributaries of the early church would have to share in such a claim! There was no isolating the Christian revelation!

Furthermore, Troeltsch did not feel in a position to promote the Christian claim of universality. He and his friends discovered the connection which exists between religious customs and doctrines, and cultural surroundings. Christianity must therefore confine itself to Western civilization, whose child it is in its most characteristic features and especially in its own concept of God.

Troeltsch did not deny the reality of God. He believed in the actuality of God. He saw him actually present in all cultural enterprises, which he interpreted as expressions of "reason," which underlies all existence. There is reason also in the life of nature, but it manifests itself most purely in history, which must

be understood as the history of culture. Man as the
agent of civilization, of history, stands in close contact with the ground of all being. *He* is closest to the
eternal. Therefore he can discern the meaning in all
that is, beholding everything concrete as a symbol of
the eternal. The concrete always contains something
eternal, but it is never the eternal itself. God, the
eternal world-reason, is immanent in all existence, and
especially in man. Revelation is where this eternal becomes conscious. This is the meaning of Troeltsch's
theory of the "religious a priori." Religion is the endeavor to relate everything to God, thus establishing
meaningfulness. The highest form of religion is then
ethical. It is the distinction of Christianity that it emphasizes the significance of the purest morality for
the establishment of true, meaningful living.

In this theology the modern world-view, particularly in its historical aspects, is frankly accepted, but
the Christian revelation has lost its unique place in
the life of man. Jesus Christ is no longer *the* revealer
of God, for everything reveals him. The Christian religion has lost its universal importance. The knowledge
of God is a natural endowment of all human beings
who seriously undertake the task of spiritualizing their
existence in all the phases of their cultural enterprise.
Religion is for Troeltsch really the confidence in the
reasonableness and the meaningfulness of the life of
the universe. It is man's distinction that he can practice this insight and become a consciously active par-
ticipant in life's process.

Troeltsch's influence was and still is tremendous.
He made himself the spokesman of many. His views
are practically identical with those held by the educated members of the middle class, especially in the

large cities, who still hold to the church. This "religion" is that of America's universities and "advanced" theological seminaries, although they hardly share in the idealistic philosophy which underlies Troeltsch's thought.

The result of our investigation is not very encouraging from a Christian point of view. The development from Schleiermacher to Troeltsch seems to indicate that the modern world-view has progressively forced the unique content of traditional Christianity into oblivion. The problem which modern theology has to face is apparently not how we must speak of God's revelation in Jesus Christ, if we cannot do it in terms of a metaphysics of supernaturalism, but whether we can speak of any kind of revelation at all.

But is there not a fact of revelation as long as people do not cease to believe in God or in "a God?" And further, has the traditional Christian belief in the absoluteness of God's revelation in Jesus Christ really been definitely disproved or found unbearable? Many people who are not at all antiquated in their thinking, still call it their own. Is it not then possible that modern theology, as it followed and follows the course that Schleiermacher laid out, has been mistaken both in method and result?

This is the question which Barth and those who have joined him raise against German theology as it has developed since the day of Schleiermacher. It is not Christianity, they say, but "modern" theology that is inadequate, particularly it is not Christian belief as expressed in the Bible and the Reformation. "God reveals himself in the Word"—this is still true today, even in the world of the Twentieth century.

Such a remarkable claim truly deserves to be ex-

amined. That is the intention of this book. In the following chapter we shall first of all investigate *how*
Barth became the prophet of the new "orthodoxy,"
and then proceed to analyse his teachings in view of
the problems with which we have just been dealing.

III

THE BEGINNING OF THE THEOLOGY OF CRISIS

KARL BARTH was born on the 10th day of May, 1886, at Basel, the son of the Rev. Fritz Barth, who later became Professor of the New Testament at the University of Bern. Here he spent his childhood, and, in 1904, entered the university. Later, he visited the German universities of Berlin, Tübingen, and Marburg. Adolph von Harnack and Wilhelm Herrmann were the teachers who influenced him most. To this day Barth considers himself a pupil of Herrmann. In a long article he explains this relationship:

"Herrmann was *the* theological teacher of my student days. I remember, as if it were today, the days when, nearly twenty years ago, I read his ethics for the first time. If I had the temperament of Klaus Harms, I could say of Herrmann something similar to what he wrote of Schleiermacher: 'I received from this book the impulse of an infinite movement.' I should like to say with more reserve but with no less gratitude: Since that time, I have paid full attention to theology. As a convinced Marburger I came to Marburg. And when, on the day when I began my first pastorate, five minutes before I went into the pulpit, the mail brought me the then

new fourth edition of the "Ethics" as a gift from
the author, I considered this coincidence as a con-
secration of the entire future. Of course, I cannot
deny that in the course of the years, I have become
a somewhat strange Herrmann pupil. . . . . . But I
could never have been willing to admit the fact of
a conversion away from Herrmann and I can not
do so to-day. What it means to be the real pupil of a
real master, generally, and particularly in regard
to theology, is a question which has not yet been
unanimously answered. But it appears to me that I
received from Herrmann something fundamental
which, thought out to all its consequences, later compelled me to say the rest differently from him and
finally to interpret even his fundamental principle
in another way. And yet, he showed it to me.
Nobody can take that from me, and I should like
gratefully to acknowledge this in public."

A wonderful tribute, indeed! We must keep it in
mind if we want to understand Barth's development.
As a Ritschlian of Herrmann's type, he began his
ministerial career. In 1909, he became assistant pastor
at the German Reformed Church in Geneva. We are
in a position to judge his frame of mind at that period,
for, in the same year, there appeared in a theological
journal an article by the young minister, entitled:
"Modern Theology and practical Church-work."[1] In
view of Barth's later development, its content is most
interesting.
    The theme of the paper is the observation that the
graduates of "liberal" theological faculties encounter
greater difficulties in beginning their practical ministry than their colleagues from "orthodox" institu-

tions. In order to explain this difficulty Barth characterizes the so-called liberal theology. Its essence is first of all *religious individualism.* "It is not obedience to laws which come to man from without, but it is meditation and concentration upon a truth which reveals itself within him." There is no universally valid source or authority of revelation which one man can prove to another. Faith is entirely personal and subjective. The second feature of modern theology is *historical relativism.* It involves the scientific examination of the sources upon which the Christian religion is founded. The literature of the New Testament is of no higher value in principle than other religious documents. Jesus as the founder of a religion is not essentially different from others. His history must be investigated by the same methods that are applied to Zoroaster or to the Avesta. Therefore: "Whosoever keeps himself to 'modern' theology must know that the question is: to be or not to be. For science deprives him of that entire historical outfit of ideas and concepts which were the 'motive and quietive' of the religion of the past; he is vigorously compelled to come to a decision about them, *i.e.,* to ask himself whether they are expressive also of his belief." In consequence, the work in the churches is not easy for such a theologian. Barth refuses to use the often recommended recipe, to throw overboard what he has learned, and to adjust himself to the milieu in which he has to work. Instead, he wants to speak to others of his individually experienced and experienceable religion, in spite of the fact that he feels himself not mature enough for such a task. "For whosoever wants to speak to others only of that which, in his own life, has become cause or effect of faith, is confronted by the Scylla of clericalism which offers more than it has, and by the Charybdis of agnosticism which offers nothing at all. But both stand threateningly before us younger theologians, and to this I attribute our immaturity, our surprisingly small enthusiasm for religious activism."

Thus, at the beginning of his career Barth was a modernist, sincerely given over to the principles and attitudes of liberal theology, but also fully aware of the dangers and responsibilities of such a position. His article was answered by two professors, who took pains to point out that the religious individualism to which the young student referred must not be identified with subjectivism, as if there were no objective truth in religion. Barth found himself compelled to speak again in self-defense.[3] He agreed with his critics in general, but eagerly and seriously affirmed that "he could not find the essence of evangelical piety in anything else but in the absolutely inward act of faith which is inaccessible to any adequate logical formulation." "God can never be an external norm. He is that individual, inner certainty and authority which in Christ as he passes through the history of men and peoples, becomes the revelation of all those who desire to be independent from an external authority."

In 1911, Barth took a pastorate in the little town of Safenwil in the Swiss canton of Aargau. That he continued to interest himself in theological questions is indicated by the publication of another article in 1914, entitled: "Belief in the Personal God."[4] The theme was not one that Barth had chosen for himself. It had been made the subject of a discussion for all Swiss ministers upon the recommendation of the Executive Committee of the Swiss Society of Ministers. The young pastor brought all his theological knowledge to bear on his topic.

He felt first of all the duty to explain why it was significant to be concerned about the problem of the personality of God. "We discover the truth of religion in its experiential content, in its experience, in its practice, in its immediacy,—to name a few of the descriptions by which we distinguish the inner factuality of the life in God from its expression in thought and ideas. Especially in regard to our problem, Schleiermacher, the father of this method in modern theology, repeatedly expresses himself to the effect that it does not make any difference to religion whether metaphysics attributes to God the predicate of personality or not, and that such a discussion is not concerned with the elements of religion but only with two different ways of considering the universe. 'In religion, the idea of God does not stand so high as you believe.' We may as well therefore spare ourselves the trouble of investigation. . . . ." But "we cannot but think and speak about the central concern of our life, about our relationship with God. The power of the immediate religious experience compels us to do so. And *if* we do so, even only fragmentarily, we are concerned with dogmatics." We must, therefore, take the work of scientific dogmatics seriously, in spite of the fact that theological thought is of secondary importance in comparison with religious experience. The scientific character of dogmatics consists in its giving as accurate an interpretation of the religious reality as possible.

After this characteristically modernistic interpretation of religion and theology the author proceeds to define "personality." He discovers three elements which constitute it: First, *Spirit*. To be a personality

means to be spirit. I am a spiritual personality in so
far as my mind, in its functions, approaches the eternal
norms of beauty, truth and goodness, and in so far
as these norms are actualized in my person.

Second, *Individuality.* This is the particular form of
the actualization of the spirit. I am a personality in so
far as I am an individual actualization of the spirit.

Thirdly, the *"I."* In "spirituality" and in "individuality," we meet only the transcendental and the
psychological forms of what constitutes personality.
They become *one* real entity in the consciousness of
self. Personality is therefore the individual, spiritual
"Self" (Ich).

In the next chapter, Barth comes, after long critical discussion of the theological thinkers of the nineteenth century, to this conclusion: "When we speak
of God's thought and will, we mean to say: He, a
definitely determined 'He,' thinks and wills. When
God makes demands of us, when he judges us and
makes us free, when we pray to him, we stand with
him in an I-thou relationship. In religion, we have
communion with a characterized individual spirit.
When religion pronounces the word God, it means
what we described as personality: an individual spiritual Self, an *absolutely* spiritual, but an *individual,*
absolutely spiritual Self." "The absolute is personality,
and a personality is the absolute."

The term "absolute" is then what denominates a
personality as divine. But this new term must be defined. In another chapter Barth takes up this task.
There he develops ideas which are dominant also in his
later writings, and which we must therefore consider
as fundamental.

"We must speak of God as free from finitude and condition as these states are necessarily connected with space and time. The polemic of A. Ritschl against the use of the term absolute in theology is justified only in so far as it opposes the one-sided emphasis upon the negativism of God made by mysticism. But it is entirely contrary to the facts when Ritschl asserts, that the absolute is not a product of religious reflection, but a metaphysical concept which is foreign to the Christian. For there is hardly a religious reflection which could really do without the negation of God's limitedness. Of course, when one takes the absolute in its liberal meaning, as being dissolved from given reality, one is guilty of a mythologoumenon. This being acquires a clear meaning only if it is understood not only as the *negative,* but also as the *positive* of all that can be thought and willed. . . . Suspension of space and time is superiority over them. . . . Pure abstractness becomes pure origin. It is the . . . truth and validity of the apriori which has proved itself the positive component of the God-idea."

These considerations, which clearly stand under the Neo-Kantian influence of the Marburg philosopher Cohen, lead Barth to look for a term which would apply to the unity of the negativeness and the positiveness which the religious experience senses when it feels itself confronted by the absolute. He chooses the concept of the "Majestic" or "Sublime." And, following R. Rothe, he emphasizes the sublime as a *neuter,* "for it must be plain that our concern is here with the *impersonal,* or if one wants to use the unhappy phrase, the *superpersonal* element in the God-idea." "Our

mind may enlarge its world of thought and will as far
as it may: God confronts it again and again as the pure
negativity of everything finite, as the supreme one who
lives in a light which no man can approach unto. But
not only is this superiority implied in this concept of
the sublime, but also the idea (Inbegriff) of sovereignty. God is absolute potency.... God is that which
makes the world, which is given to our mind, absolutely possible. We thus arrive at the paradoxical fact
that the same one who lives in a light which no man
can approach unto, is not far from every one of us;
in him we live and move and have our being. The concept of the sublime comprises both the transcendence
and the immanence of God. His transcendence is his
absolute superiority, his immanence his absolute sovereignty."

The conclusion of all these speculations is that the
sentence "God is absolute personality" means "God
is sublime personality." The question now arises
whether it is possible to speak of a sublime personality,
particularly if "personality" is understood as an individual spiritual "I" or "self." That the concepts of
sublimity and of spirituality do not exclude each other
can clearly be seen. But does the conception of a "self"
permit itself to be connected with that of the "sublime?" Is a "sublime" self thinkable? Evidently not,
for an individuality of absolute potency is inconceiv-
able. If one emphasizes the *sublimity* of God, one can
no longer assert his individual selfhood. One then approaches *Pantheism*. But, Barth maintains, religious
experience protests against such a trend, and insists on
being in a relationship with a "thou."

We become entangled in still another difficulty if
we stress the *individuality* of God over against his sub-

limity. For the concept of individuality necessarily implies a "not yet" or "not yet totally." We would have to maintain a limited sublimity of God, and would thus arrive at *Deism,* a belief which does not do justice to religious experience. Religious experience, Barth insists, demands the *togetherness* of the "sublime" *and* the "personal" in God. They cannot be thought together logically, but in spite of logical incongruity, they belong together. But where is that inner necessity on the basis of which this claim can be made in the name of the religious experience?

Barth refers to the attempt of the philosophers *Siebeck* and especially *Lotze* (who, it may be noted incidentally, influenced Bowen, the founder of the religious philosophy of *Personalism*) to ascertain the validity of a personal God concept by the evidence of the human personality. The human personality, the individual-spiritual self, the personalists argue, is the most sublime thing we know of—therefore, the sublime itself must be personal. But this kind of reasoning, Barth believes, is not permissible. The criticism that Ludwig Feuerbach advanced against religion would then be valid. This philosopher presented the theory that the God-belief of the religions is a grand illusion, and God nothing else but the projection of anthropomorphic ideas into the realm of the transcendent. If Lotze's idea were accepted, it would be difficult to refute Feuerbach's suspicion that the secret of all religion is egoism.

Barth therefore comes to the following conclusion: "The God-idea of religion cannot be something that we have projected from *ourselves,* but only the reflection of a fact which has been created in us. This fact is the life which is given us by God and mediated to us through history. Our being conditioned by history is our religious experience. In it we have God, and on this basis we can speak of God. From it we have taken the elements of the God-idea which we have described; the reason for the strange antinomy of these elements, therefore, must be found in this experience. It should be possible to demonstrate this antinomy in any kind of religious experience, but we refer to that life from God which has become effective in history in the gospel of Jesus. The inner contrast which leads to the antinomy in the God-concept has here found its deepest, most complete and clearest expression."

He then proceeds to show that the gospel is centered around two main ideas. It emphasizes the eternal worth of the human soul, personality, and it preaches the Kingdom of God. These two factors, seemingly incongruous, constitute the teaching of the Christian gospel. "We are told to call upon God as children call upon their father, but we are also advised to deny ourselves and to make God's honor, God's Kingdom, God's will, the object of our prayer." "The attitude of man in view of the coming Kingdom is described in words which are again and again incomprehensible—'that the soul must be lost for the sake of the gospel,' in order to be saved—and these words are to be found in Mark immediately preceding the saying regarding the 'eternal value of the human soul.' Does all this not border on the impossible thought that the true destiny of the personality is its complete surrender to the cause which it should serve?" Thus there is in the religious experience of the gospel the antinomy which constitutes the God-idea, the antinomy between personality and sublimity.

We have recorded the theological thought of Barth

in the year of 1914, because its expression in this essay
on the personality of God will help us to understand
his message of later years, which was to bring him
into the bright light of public attention. Furthermore,
this article has been overlooked by the critics and re-
viewers of the later Barth, though it gives us significant hints of the particular trend of his mind.
Without attempting to undertake a psychological
analysis of a man who is still among the living—and
very actively so!—and who, with irony and laughter,
could refute any suggestion we might advance—and
how the thinkers of the past would laugh at our historical analyses of their thought, if they could!—we
must yet be permitted to call attention to certain emphases which later on came to the front in a new theology. In this article of 1914, Barth is certainly still under the powerful influence of Herrmann: he stresses
individual religious experience; he makes the experience of the historical Jesus authoritative for the knowledge of God. These things are not here of primary
interest to us, but the eagerness and passion with which
the young theologian points out the majestic, sublime,
humanly inaccessible traits in God should be noted
clearly. Furthermore, one should remember the surprising readiness with which he accepts Feuerbach's
criticism of religion and of all anthropomorphic God-
concepts, a readiness which does not well agree with
the ease with which he presents his own argument.
For does he not himself make the God-concept of a
sublime personality plausible by pointing to the human
experiences revealed in the gospels?   Again, in his
description of evangelical religion he evinces much
more enthusiasm for its demand of absolute surrender

to the divine cause than for its high evaluation of human personality.

Five years later, the same young theologian found himself suddenly made famous by his publication of a commentary on Paul's letter to the Romans. We do not know much of his activity during the years between 1914 and 1918. It is said that he was then a religious socialist under the influence of the Swiss pastor Kutter, who in the name of Christian religion criticized the Church for its conformity to the world in organization and ethics. A lecture which Barth delivered in January 1916 at Aarau and which is printed in his first volume of collected essays, indicates that he then shared such an opinion. Under the title "The Righteousness of God," he condemns Western civilization for having substituted the righteousness of man for that of God. Disregarding and disobeying the strict voice of conscience, Western Man has erected a Tower of Babel. Barth comes to this conclusion:[5] "In the question, Is God Righteous? our whole Tower of Babel falls to pieces. In this burning question, it becomes evident that we are looking for a righteousness without God, that we are looking in truth for a god without God and against God—and that our quest is hopeless. It is clear that such a god is not God. He is not even righteous. He cannot prevent his worshipers, all the distinguished European and American apostles of civilization, welfare and progress, all zealous citizens and pious Christians, from falling upon one another with fire and sword to the amazement and derision of the poor heathen in India and Africa. This god is really an unrighteous god, and it is high time for us to declare ourselves thorough-going doubters, sceptics, scoffers and atheists in regard to him. It is high time for us to confess freely and gladly: this god, to whom we have built the Tower of Babel, is not God. He is an idol. He is dead." By being still and letting conscience speak, he suggests, we shall hear God's righteousness and not one that we as men wish for or determine. "It will then be, above all, a matter of our recognizing God once more as God. It is easy to say recognize. But recognizing is an ability won only in fierce inner personal conflict. It is a task beside which all cultural, moral and patriotic duties, all efforts in 'applied religion' are child's play. For here one must give himself up in order to give himself over to God, that God's will be done. To do his will, however, means to begin with him anew. His will is not a corrected continuation of our own. It approaches one as a Wholly Other. There is nothing for our will except a basic re-creation." [6]

The voice which speaks here is new and strong. It is the voice of a prophet, who warns his fellow-believers in God's name to abstain from choosing the wrong path in religious matters. It is the voice of a man who opposes the doings of the good, pious, religious people, because he feels that in all their goodness they do not recognize God as God.

It was this same voice which rang in the pages of the Commentary on the Epistle to the Romans, making everyone listen who had ears with which to hear. This book, brought out by a more or less locally limited publishing house, [7] quickly found its way into all German-speaking countries. It was eagerly studied and discussed. It differed from ordinary exegetical works. It acknowledged the insight gained by historical research, but was far from being a historical commentary. Taking it for granted, that Paul as a child of his time spoke to his contemporaries, Barth attempted to show that, as a prophet and apostle of the Kingdom of God, he spoke to all men of all times. His entire attention was directed toward the eternal spirit of the Bible in and beyond that which is merely historical. The strong voice of Paul was made to be heard in our time, his questions and answers interpreted as our questions and answers.

In the Preface, Barth confesses to having written the book in the joy of a discovery. And, truly, there is a sweeping enthusiasm in his sentences. The academic critics called his work a collection of sermons rather than a scholarly achievement. But Barth had no pretensions to scholarship. He spoke as a man who had found something in Paul, something hitherto unknown to himself, and he made Paul speak not to Greeks and Jews but to the theologians and church people of the twentieth century. Equipped with an astonishing knowledge of the world's literature, endowed with the critical wisdom of a theologian conversant with the profoundities of *religions* and religious thinkers, gifted with a remarkable power of analysis of the contemporary movements of civilization, fully aware of the baffling problems of Western culture, the author of this commentary lets Paul preach to our own time. The world of the ancient Jews becomes the world of the Twentieth Century—and the righteousness of God as the gospel portrays it is brought to bear on this world. Recognize God as God!—that is the message. Take the *reality* of God seriously—that is the command. Paul (Barth[8] is an anti-Idealist, for the Idealist lives in ideas and not in realities) — is concerned about his idealities, not about God in his *reality*. He is an anti-subjectivist, for "truth lies in the objective." He is an anti-pietist, for inner experiences are a horror to him. He is an anti-liberal, for liberalism humanizes, adjusts to history and psychology what cannot be adjusted. He is an anti-fundamentalist, because neither dogma nor Bible-book are *real*. And all this opposition for the sake of *divine realism* and universalism. "We do not," he says,[9] "depend upon a religious theory, ... still less do we lean upon the breakable staff of so-called religious experiences. We deal with reality, with the emergence of the essential truth of life, with the breakdown of an old bond comprehending all mankind, with the opening of a new life-content which includes all mankind, yea, the world. We deal with God." With God as he has become real in Jesus Christ, we should add. "He is that which religion and morality drive toward, in which they are overcome. He is the righteousness of God which now has come into power."

Forgotten is the emphasis on religious experience, religious individualism, and historical relativism, the voice of conscience—and all the authorities upon which Barth had formerly based his belief and theology. Everything is now concentrated upon the one great cosmic reality of God as it has revealed itself in Christ —not in the historical Jesus, but in the Christ in whom Paul and the apostles believed. Human motives, intentions, experiences, personalities and individualities— every type of subjectivity become insignificant. They are illusions in the face of the one and only reality: God. This is the new discovery. This is the beginning of the new theology which has drawn the attention of the entire Christian world to itself.

What had happened? We cannot explain it better than in Barth's own words. He answered the question in an address [10] to his fellow ministers: "For twelve

years, I was a minister, as all of you are. I *had* my
theology. It was not really mine, to be sure, but that
of my unforgotten teacher Wilhelm Herrmann,
grafted upon the principles which I had learned less
consciously than unconsciously in my native home—
the principles of the Reformed Churches. . . . Once
in the ministry, I found myself growing away from
those theological habits of thought and being forced
back at every point more and more upon the specific
minister's problem, the *sermon*. I sought to find my
way between the problem of human life on the one
hand and the content of the Bible on the other. As
a minister, I wanted to speak to the *people* in the infinite contradiction of their life, but to speak the no
less infinite message of the *Bible* which was as much
of a riddle as life. Often enough these two magnitudes,
life and the Bible, have risen before me (and still rise)
like Scylla and Charybdis: if these are the whence and
the whither of Christian preaching, who shall, who can
be a minister and preach. . . . ."

". . . . It simply came about that the familiar situation of the minister on Saturday at his desk and on
Sunday in his pulpit crystallized in my case into a marginal note to all theology, which finally assumed the
voluminous form of a complete commentary on the
Epistle to the Romans . . . I finally went to work upon
the Epistle to the Romans, which first was to be only an
essay to help me to know my own mind. Naturally and
evidently there are many subjects mentioned in the
book—New Testament theology, dogmatics, ethics
and philosophy—but you will best understand it when
you hear through it all the ministers' question: what is
preaching?—not, how *does* one do it? but how *can*
one do it? . . . And so there grew what threatens now

to broaden out somewhat into 'my theology' or let us say, a 'corrective theology.' "

The "corrective" theology thus developed in the mind of a pastor whose task of preaching baffled him. Facing the expectant faces of his congregation, wondering *why* and for what they had come, seeing the open Bible on pulpit and altar, he had not the courage to speak about his own thoughts and feelings or preach about *his* theology. The questioning in the eyes of the people, who had come to *church* in order to have their question answered—not by the human wisdom of a more or less well trained minister!—and the problem of the open Bible, so silent and yet so pressing—these compelled this minister to forget *his* theology and philosophy and forced upon him a new analysis of the meaning of life and a new study of the Scripture. Thus he became aware of the awful reality of *God,* in the thought of whom his soul had vibrated, as his earlier theological essays reveal. The objectivity of the majestic, sublime God, of the divine sovereignty, overcame him. It was this unspeakable reality, he felt, to which the questions of his congregation pointed. It was this reality which hovered about the pages of the sacred book. The men of the Bible, the prophets, apostles, did not act like modern preachers. They did not speak about their own feelings, inner experiences. They did not write biographies, indulged in no hero-worship. They did not even speak about religion— their distinctive mark is that they stood in contrast and conflict to what is called religious practice and religious history. "Biblical piety is conscious of its own limits, of its relativity. In its essence it is humility, fear of the Lord. It points beyond the world, and points at the same time and above all beyond itself. It lives ab-

solutely by virtue of its object and for its object."
"Always there is the same seeing of the invisible, the
same hearing of the inaudible, the same incomprehensible but no less undeniable epidemic of standing still
and looking up." "The Bible lifts us out of the old
atmosphere of men to the open portals of a new world,
the world of God." [11]

We are in a position to supplement Barth's own
description of the conversion which caused him to become the leader of a new theological movement, by
another report. His helpmate, Eduard Thurneysen,
engaged in a discussion with the leader of the Swiss
religious socialists, Prof. Ragaz, once gave the following account of the experiences and factors which led
him and his friend Barth into the new venture: [12]

"Not far from here lies Safenwil and still a little
farther away Leutwil, where, during the years of
the war, Karl Barth and I were ministers. Both of
us were religious socialists—as one had to be in those
days, if the appeal of the times, and the needs and
enterprises of his generation had awakened him
from ecclesiastical slumber. Socialism, connected
perhaps with temperance, was the movement that
was to us the most impressive parable, if not the
substance, of the Kingdom of God, which we
preached on Sundays. And the task of preaching
was in those days our central concern. Then came
the war. At its outbreak we recognized first of all
a judgment upon that Christianity which had identified itself altogether too much with bourgeois interests. But the more decisively the deluge of the
war broke down everything that was seemingly built
firm and high, the more we saw the ruin not only

of the bourgeois-Christian but also of the religious-social ideology. Not only the great 'isms' at our right, nationalism and militarism, but also the 'isms' at our left, especially socialism, came under the crisis.

"A huge, yawning abyss opened before us. And if we may call the bourgeois, socialistic, ecclesiastical and religious interpretations of the meaning of the events of the times, the bridges which were brought to cross the abyss, we must say that they all proved much too short. They all fell into the pit. . . . .

"In this situation something very simple happened to us: Our attention was presently called to the Bible. . . . We had known it, oh, to be sure, we had known it before—but we had read it through the glasses of certain interpretations. These interpretations broke up in the same way that the theology and world-view broke up which had produced and sustained them. Now we read the Bible in a new way, with much fewer reservations than before. I do not dare say without any; for if that really happened, things would look still more different. We read it (I dare say *this!*) more respectfully, more as an eternal word addressed to us and to our times. We criticized it less. We did not seek in it our bourgeois or socialistic, critical or conservative opinions. We read it with the eyes of shipwrecked people whose everything had gone overboard.

"The Bible appeared in a new light. Beyond all interpretations its genuine word began to speak again: the word of the forgiveness of sins, the gospel of the coming Kingdom, coming not from men but from God. . . . .

"In the midst of this encounter with the Bible, Barth's letter to the Romans was written. From that

time on we have occupied ourselves with the great
actual truth which lies hidden in the old abused
terms: Word of God, church, sin, grace, justification
by faith, return of Christ, reconciliation, redemption. The Bible led us back to the Reformation, and
the Bible and the Reformation have held our attention throughout the years."

What is the meaning of all this? Is it an expression
of war-psychology? This is a frequent interpretation
of Barthian theology. By saying that Barthianism is
nothing but a reaction to the war, critics have tried to
dismiss it as a temporary phenomenon. But that is a
pitifully superficial opinion. Yes, the dialectical theology was born in the war and in consequence of it. But
that does not make it a temporary concern. For the
war, as a matter of fact, compelled everyone to reorient
himself in the most radical fashion. Only now we are
beginning fully to realize that a new period in history
began, when the war was finally ended. The whole
world is still in convulsion, trying in vain to make a
readjustment. All nations are groping in the dark,
waiting and looking for the new day. Even America
has finally awakened to the awareness that the foundation of human existence was universally shaken by the
events of the years 1914-1918.

The disillusionment has been slow in coming, but it
finally has come, and it will grow upon us still more
cruelly, when the shouts of panic and the frantic and
hysterical cries for help are replaced by a calm consideration of the real causes of the modern situation.
We shall then continue to discuss the problems of dis-
armament and pacifism, of reparations, war-debts and
unemployment, of Bolshevism and Socialism—but we

shall no longer tackle them solely under the aspect of human possibility, as if an effective application of our human abilities and methods could solve them. We shall continue to meditate upon the merits of science and the machine, upon humanism and human organization, upon the social program and the building of a better world—but much less confidently than heretofore shall we trust in the ultimate value of our human efforts. For all of us will have to pass through the depths of disillusionment. Particularly we shall learn to hesitate to consider these things religious issues, the issues of God.

Perhaps we shall then be able to appreciate how the war could disillusion Barth and his friends about the ultimate value of the causes to which they had lent their religious energies. They became aware of the fact that God, if he really is, cannot be identical with any cause or program which man embraces for the sake of his control over life. The turmoil of the war had rendered all these programs questionable, insofar as they claimed any absolute significance. Idealisms which could break so easily could not be identified with God. But God, if he were God, was discovered as the totally Other, the unshakable reality, in no way one with any cause or attitude of the world of man. The Bible, which had been called upon to sanction the social messianism and the cultural optimism of the pre-war period, was now seen in an entirely new light. Barth observed that the prophets and apostles had done just what he felt to be his own duty. They had pointed to the reality of God. They had not been primarily concerned with human experiences, with human enterprises, but with God in his absolute reality, to whom every human undertaking must adjust itself, in whose light every human value becomes relative.

At the beginning of the Barthian theology stands therefore the *message of the reality of God*, and the Bible is understood as a collection of documents which incessantly point to this fact, that God alone can be considered real, absolute, sovereign.

This was the background of the strange power in this untheological theological commentary. It was sensed by all who read it. To be sure, the critics were numerous; but to many it was a relief and a salvation. The question which had forced the pen into the fingers of the student Barth to explain why modernist theologians found it more difficult to preach with authority than their orthodox brethren, had oppressed the minds of many a young minister. The same Barth, so it seemed, now spoke the saving word. He seemed to show the way into a new realization of the Christian belief in God. Perhaps he was to be the prophet of a new era in Protestantism, an era which, recognizing the value of the findings of critical scientific research in history and philosophy, would return to the strong religious faith of the Reformers. The gap between modernism and orthodoxy would be bridged. The dissolution of Protestantism due to its altogether too great readiness to adjust itself to the modern world would be arrested. The longing of many an open doubter and of many a secret and reticent sceptic for a new consciousness of God, for a new realization of God's revelation, would be fulfilled.

Academic theology did not consider the new contribution of any great value. It recognized the earnestness of the author's intention, but generally condemned him. He had written no commentary at all.

Disregarding all well established methods of scientific exegesis, he had imposed his own ideas upon the words of Paul, using the literary form of a commentary for the expression of his own theological thought. And even his own ideas were lacking in clarity. What was Barth's intention? one asked. Did he propose a return to Biblicism or to orthodoxy? And on what authority could he preach his gospel of a rediscovered God? Was he just another heretic who, leaving the path of orderly ministerial and theological conduct, propagandized a pessimistic religiousness, mistaking it for true Christianity?

IV

THE DEVELOPMENT OF THE DIALECTICAL THEOLOGY

THREE years after the *Commentary on the Romans* was published a second edition appeared. It had been completely rewritten. In it the core of the "theology of crisis," of the "Barthian theology," for the first time took definite shape; the author spoke with more self-confidence than before. His criticism had become more incisive, the sweep of his thought mightier; and he presented still more provocatively than before, his central interest in the Pauline theology.

We shall fully discuss the matured Barthian message as it appeared in this second edition, in another chapter. Here, we must confine ourselves to general characterizations, as we are primarily interested in Barth's theological development. In the Preface, the significant facts are mentioned by Barth himself. He defends himself first of all against those critics who called him an enemy of historical criticism. And he defends by attacking.

Declaring the common exegetical methods insufficient, he describes the usual procedure in the following words:[1] The exegetes of the Biblical text "are satisfied with an interpretation which I cannot call an interpretation, but only the first primitive attempt at one. They are satisfied with establishing the text by

translating and transcribing the Greek words and
phrases into the corresponding modern ones, by phil-
ological and archaeological interpretations of the results thus gained, and by a more or less plausible coordi-
nation of the single results with a historical and psychological pragmatism. . . ." "I am always astonished at
the modesty of their demands when I consider how
they have labored for proper understanding and interpretation. I call that proper understanding and interpretation which Luther with intuitive skill gave
us in his commentaries, and which Calvin in his exegesis seems systematically to have striven for . . ." The
true method of exegesis, as Barth sees it, is, therefore,
one which will succeed in making the wall between the
First and the Twentieth Centuries transparent, until
the man of the Twentieth Century can hear what Paul
speaks, "until the conversation between document
and reader is completely concentrated upon the *object* (which *must* be one and the same for each). I,
the exegete, must come to that point where I am aware
of the riddle of the object rather than of the riddle of
the document; where I, therefore, nearly forget that
I am not the author, where I have understood him
nearly so well that I can let him speak in my name and
I can speak in his."

The significance of these statements is not their revolt against the insufficiency and inadequacy of the
so-called scientific method of Biblical exegesis, but
the assertion that the interest of the Biblical books is
no different from that of the modern man. This assumption on Barth's part is astonishing. Have we not
been taught that the world-views of the early Christians were totally foreign to us; and have we not been
led to believe that our difficulties in remaining Chris-

tian are due to a radical change in our conception of the world and of life? Does Barth, then, mean to say that this opinion so universally held by "educated" men, is unjustified? His repeated assertion that the doctrine of the literal inspiration of the Bible is not easily to be pushed aside, may mean just this; yet, he himself has clearly stated that he would not think of defending this opinion, for he admits the principal validity of the methods of historical criticism.

The solution of the problem as he sees it, is given in the following quotation: "God is in heaven and you are on earth. The relation of *this* God with *this* man, the relation of *this* man with *this* God is for me the theme of the Bible as well as the substance of philosophy." In other words: the Bible and modern philosophy cannot disagree in so far as both start from, or arrive at the same conclusion that man cannot live without God, *without God who is in heaven!* Man cannot save himself; he cannot be the master of his life. In all such striving he will finally arrive at the point where he, as man, goes bankrupt, where he must surrender to what can only be beyond the realm of human grasp or capacity: to God, the wholly Other. It is this that Barth and his friends have called the "crisis." It begins when humanistic philosophies and religions are found lacking, when systems of thought and ethics, in so far as they depend upon the validity or sufficiency of human reason, fail to supply man with the absolute certainty of the meaning of life. It is the old, old question of certainty which is in the background of the Barthian theology. That man cannot depend upon himself, upon his human experiences, when this need is aroused—this is the discovery in which Barth rejoiced when he wrote his commentary on the *Epistle to the Romans.* The problem of the men of the Bible and of the Twentieth Century is the same, because men of all times must admit the futility of their endeavor to control life and fill it with absolute meaning. Man is compelled always to look into a "Yonder" when he desires to know the "whence" and "whither" of his existence. He *must* admit: "God is in heaven and I am on earth." He must let God be God. He cannot wrest from God what belongs to him by claiming that he, out of himself and from his own resources, could give life absolute meaning.

This is the theme of Barth's theology and the root of his alleged Biblicism. The Bible deals with the perennial human problem of the meaning of life. To understand and to interpret it is to enter into a conversation with the men of the Bible about this problem. Because they approached the subject with the utmost earnestness, they must be taken seriously. And if they know its solution, they must be heard. It is a fact that they claimed to *know* this solution; indeed, they lived by the belief that in Jesus Christ eternal life was attainable because God had revealed himself in him. Shall we, therefore, not listen to their testimony? Will it not also be possible for us to understand their belief well enough to make it our own, so that we, too, may believe that Jesus Christ is God's revelation?

Barth came to this conviction and became the founder of a new theology. One may ask, what is *new* in this teaching? Has not the Christian Church cherished this faith throughout the centuries? Has it not always taught that Jesus Christ is the way and the truth and the life? Yes, Barth would answer, Christianity *has* kept the faith of the Bible, but in a way which has defiled it, for it has too often forgotten that

God is God. It has transformed God's revelation into
a human possession or attitude. It has ignored the
crisis of man. This charge must be raised particularly
against modern Protestantism, which has substituted
human experiences and inner feelings—psychological
facts—for God's authority, which can never be
human. The same criticism can be made against Orthodoxy and Fundamentalism, since they erroneously
identify the authority of God with that of a book or
of a doctrine. Nor can Catholicism, either, claim to
represent pure Christianity, for it relies upon supernature for the attainment of the divine, and even supernature, *if* it can be attained, is not *God who is in
heaven*. Barth's "Biblicism" involves a turning away
from nearly all types of Christian theology and an *attack* upon them all, in the name of the God in whom
Paul and the Apostles believed.

The commentary on the *Epistle of the Romans* is,
therefore, an exceedingly critical book. Paul's arguments for Christ, which in the First Century were directed against the Jews and Gentiles of the ancient
world, are now aimed at the Christians of the Twentieth Century. In Barth's interpretation, the Apostle
becomes a warrior who carries the banner of God, the
"Wholly Other," against the pious Christians, who
assume the role of *creatores creatoris*, creators of the
Creator. "God's righteousness versus human righteousness"—this Pauline refrain, which more than once,
when rediscovered and reapplied, has resulted in re-
volts and reformations within the church of Christ,
is the theme of the Barthian theology of crisis.

No wonder that Barth feels closely related to those
before him who had been engaged in similar enterprises. The reformers, Luther and Calvin (the latter

especially), are often quoted by him as his masters and teachers. He affiliates himself also, it is particularly interesting to note, with those solitary figures of recent times that have raised warning or critical voices against the churches; and in consequence have been ignored as irritating outsiders. Barth resurrected Kierkegaard, Overbeck and Dostoievsky, discovering in them spirits akin to himself.

Much has been said, particularly since the second edition of his *Commentary on the Romans,* of Barth's references to *Kierkegaard.* He adopted some of his terminology, especially the dialectical concept of "time and eternity." Barth once said:[2] "If I have a system, it is this, that I keep in mind as strictly as possible what Kierkegaard called the infinite qualitative difference between time and eternity, both in its positive and negative meaning." That is only another way of saying that God is God and not man. When Barth frequently refers to the infinite contrast between time and eternity, we should not at once jump to the conclusion that his theology was inspired by Kierkegaard. It is still more erroneous to maintain that Barth's Paulinism is nothing but a metaphysical system, based on the paradoxical contrast between time and eternity.

Of similar significance is *Overbeck.* This fervent critic of modern Protestant thought, who opposed the self-confidence with which theological scholars assumed the accuracy of their modernizing analyses and findings, taught Barth to be even more critical than the Modernists. He opened his eyes to the unapproachable remoteness of God and to the delicateness of theological expression which hints at the divine rather than speaks of it directly.

Dostoievsky, the writer of human tragedies, the

painter of human lowliness and perverseness, became a "godfather" to Barthianism for a similar reason. He had wanted to be a Christian poet. And as a man with a profound understanding of the meaning of the Cross, he put halos around the heads of those pitiable individuals, the outcasts of mankind, whom he depicted in his novels. Barth himself had come upon the same truth.

The second edition of Barth's famous book had a still greater influence. Although he disclaimed any intention of introducing a new theological system, he was considered by many the founder of a new school of theology. In 1921, he was called to the chair of Reformed Theology at the University of Göttingen, where he developed his "corrective" theology into a system. Four years later he was called to the University of Münster, Westphalia; and in 1929 to Bonn.

His success as a professor was amazing. Students came from all over Germany to hear him. His book called forth a deluge of critical literature, and his ideas were discussed on all sides. An increasing number of the young theologians have been drawn into his camp; and, although there is hardly one who is willing to adopt completely the Barthian terminology or to follow *exactly* his trend of thought, he has been a stimulus and inspiration to them and given them a new outlook on their work in theology and the church. Today one speaks of a "Barthian school." The names of Professors Brunner (Zürich), Bultmann (Marburg), Gogarten (Breslaŭ) are as well known as that of Barth himself; while many other theological teachers and ministers are said to be in sympathy with Barthian ideas.

Barth's work became, of necessity, more academic after assuming his professorship, but it would be wrong to assume that on that account he lost his original fervor and enthusiasm. On the contrary, he followed, with surprising energy and amazing industry, the course which he had laid out for himself. His public lectures, which appeared in the bi-monthly journal of the Barthian school, published under the significant title, "Between the Eras," and which were brought out later in book form, indicate clearly his constant preoccupation with the history of Christian thought and the life of the present-day church. The most recent volume, in particular, entitled *Theology and the Church*, is practically a review of the history of Protestant thought under the aspect of the theology of crisis.

It remains for us to consider three other books of Barth which were published during the period of his work in Göttingen and Münster. Two of them are commentaries on Paul's letters to the Corinthians and to the Philippians. They stand in line with the famous *Commentary on the Romans*. They, also, are reprints of academic lectures. The third is the first volume of a system of theology or dogmatics.

The interpretation of I. *Cor.*, which is really an exposition of the Fifteenth Chapter in connection with the preceding ones—is entitled "The Resurrection of the Dead," and is another example of the theological exegesis which Barth had inaugurated in contrast, or rather in corrective addition, to the methods of historical criticism. He argues here much more calmly than in his previous work. The preaching of Paul is not so directly, as before, presented as a radical attack upon Twentieth Century Christianity. Paul appears here less modern, but certainly no less actual. In many ways this commentary contains an even more acute and severe criticism of Christianity, for Barth makes the interesting and certainly quite convincing attempt to show that Paul's discussion of various practical and very local Corinthian matters and problems is not at all as casual as the exegetes so commonly suppose. He points out that Paul's review of Corinthian affairs— the factions, the controversy regarding gentile courts, the problems of marriage and sexual life, prevailing customs, rules of social behavior, *etc.*—is from one central point of view and that he argues in each single case against one principal attitude, namely against the development of a *Christian* "world," as if Christian faith must needs result in a fixed set of habits and regulations, in which the reality, or rather the actuality, of God would have ceased to be the acute crisis of all life including "Christian" life. On the basis of *this* interpretation of the letter as a unity, the fifteenth chapter is then understood as its crowning argument. Here, Paul finally reveals what has lain in back of his mind as he has brought the Corinthian misinterpretations of Christianity one by one before the tribunal of his apostleship: the belief in the resurrection of the dead, the resurrection of the *body*.

What Barth presents in this connection as Pauline thought differs widely from almost everything that has ever been said about it, and yet he seems to have grasped the real underlying meaning and theological truth. It is unbelievable how modern this Paul appears in his argument with the Christian doubters: he seems to share the scruples and finesse of a sophisticated modern man who has analyzed the problem of God in all possible directions. To the historian of the New Testament, such a Paul may be nothing but a caricature, but to the historian of Christian thought he is surely no impossibility. In more than one decisive period in the history of the church, men have derived from Paul's words a wisdom which previous ages had never been able to discover in them. It was not Paul of Tarsus—who probably died in Rome between 62 and 64 A. D.—who argued in the writings of Augustine against the Pelagians, and in the pamphlets of Luther against the papal schoolmen of the Middle Ages; but it was certainly the same spirit (πνεῦμα) which gave to this Christ-converted Jew his "apostolic" message for the ancient world, and to the later leaders their messages. Why should not this same "spirit" have been revived in Barth himself against the secularization of modern Christianity? This, at least, is what he intimates in his theological exegesis.

For Barth, therefore, the Pauline discussion of the resurrection of the body is only a particularly striking way of presenting the crisis of God, under which all life stands. To preach the resurrection of the body means to preach God as he *actually* is; to believe it, means to live a life which is qualified by that love which, according to I Cor. 13, springs from an eschatological knowledge which is none other than that by which we are known. It involves the change from the *cogito ergo sum* to the *cogitor ergo sum,* the change from a man who will not admit the absolute finality, limitedness and finiteness of his existence, to a man who has been overcome by the realization that he must die and with him his universe (even granted it has stood and will stand for billions and billions of years), one who has thus received a new qualification for his existence because he has beheld an ultimate reality, as profoundly contrary to finite reality as eternity is to time.

In the mind of Barth, the resurrection of the dead has nothing to do with immortality or with a life beyond physical death. "The resurrection of the dead" is a purely religious term, which signifies that invisible and unspeakably radical change in the *quality* of human existence, and of existence in general, which it receives when its limitedness, its definite restriction by the fact of death, is realized. The abyss of meaning*less*ness which then opens before us, reveals at the same time a profundity of meaning*ful*ness. Death discloses the void and at the same time the eternal. It is only in the face of nothingness that life receives its *eternal* value. Such is the *resurrection* of the dead, as Barth understands it. It is also the God-idea as he conceives it. It is in the radical and thorough awareness of the inescapable limitedness of his experience that man comes to a recognition of the supreme value of it. What seems like an absolute negation is, as a matter of fact, a most positive affirmation. Death is the gate of resurrection. Only that life which has faced death, only that life which does not attempt to circumvent or avoid death, is sacred, saved, safe. And that which in death and from beyond death brings about this salvation, is *God*. In that sense, belief in the resurrection of the body, of the dead, is another name for God.

Barth's theology—or shall we say his religious philosophy?—finds in this idea its most profound expression. It is a conception not at all foreign to the philosophies and religions of mankind. Barth, himself, has set forth similar ideas in his article on the personality of God which we analyzed in the last chapter. Under the evident influence of the Neo-Kantian Cohen, he spoke of the "origin," meaning thereby the "absolute" in its negative and positive sense. In his *Commentary on the Romans* as well as in the book of the *Resurrection of the Dead* (and as a matter of fact, in all his writings) he often uses the terms "God" and "Origin" as synonymous. In the light of these reflections, we can understand better what he meant to say, when he wrote: " 'God is in heaven and you are on earth.' The relation of *this* God with *this* man, the relation of *this* man with *this* God is for me the theme of the Bible as well as the substance of philosophy. The philosophers call this crisis in human knowledge the origin. The Bible sees at this focal point Jesus Christ." Through Jesus Christ, in Barth's opinion, men like Paul came to the belief in the "resurrection of the body," in "God," in the "origin." We have just explained what the meaning of all this is. These ideas, and all the connotations which they imply, are either supremely profound or supremely absurd. This is just the manner in which Barth wants them understood; for he is clearly conscious of the fact that faith in God, as the Bible preaches it, is possible only to one who has frankly and squarely faced the fact that he must die. Such a faith will, therefore, seem impossible and foolish to one who thinks that he can live unmindful of the *end* of his existence. Those who eat, drink, and are merry are outside of God, the real God, who reveals Himself exactly at the death-line. Outside of God also are all those who hold ideas and beliefs which help them to avoid facing the finality of death, such as those who believe in immortality as personal survival after death, those who worship the progress of the race, or the builders of ideologies which deal with life as if it were perennial, *everlasting*, deathless, and which fail to point out the true sacredness of every concrete existence that lasts from birth to death, and possesses in this very limitedness the *quality* of eternity. Barth's criticism of modern theology arises from his conviction that it has allowed Christianity—at least partially—to become enveloped in systems and attitudes of this sort, thereby losing the direct vividness of the belief in God which caused Paul to write his letters.

The book on the *Resurrection of the Dead* is significant for the understanding of the development of Barth's thinking, as it brings out clearly what he is most earnestly concerned with. It is a curious interpretation of the belief in the resurrection that he presents, one that goes back behind the literal meaning of the words and behind their historical connotation and setting; but who would say that it is a misinterpretation? Perhaps Paul is better understood than he understood himself. Barth may here point out a meaning which is valid beyond time and space. Granted that this "theological exegesis" may easily open the door to arbitrariness, that its methods are by no means clearly discernible, yet it can not be denied that its results are significant.

As an illustration of this, and as a summary of our discussion of the *Commentary on the Corinthians,* consider the following quotation:[3] "The word 'resurrection of the dead' is for him (Paul) doubtless nothing but a transcription of the word 'God.' What else could the Easter-gospel be but the very concrete message that God is Lord! It is necessary, however, to transcribe this message into the concrete. God is Lord: in this general form one might interpret the message as signifying God's sovereignty over the world, over nature and history, and with this very pious thought dodge God. I am not the world, or nature, or

history. If I know only this God, I know only as much
as I can know of fate. I can be concerned about this
God only as an expectant, non-participating spectator.
God is the Lord of *life*. This is more concrete; but this
might suggest the measureless life of the world as *we*
know it. But in this measureless life, my life is lost as
a drop in the sea. The idea that the universe is conditioned by God is certainly a pious thought, but it is
surely not a thought which would fully claim *me* for
God. God is *spirit* and as such he is the Lord. One might
derive therefrom the idea that God is Lord in *His*
world, a world of spirit, but that *we* are left to ourselves in our earthly world. God would then be our
Lord only in so far as we participated in the spirit,
in so far as we are *spirit*. But how questionable, how
narrow and meager, how restricted is our spiritualness,
even if one admits its reality. And what about the rest
of our being, that which is evidently *not* spirit, but
earth, body? God is Lord of the *body!* Now the question of God becomes acute and unescapable. Man is
body. *I* am body, and I, as this man, am God's. Now at
last I can no longer hide from God, or use a dualism as
a pretext, or retreat into a reality which would be safe
from him, or excuse myself because of earthly weakness. If God is Lord, he is Lord of that which is earthly
in me. Just that is meant. I am that which is earthly—
and as such I am to live in God. The spirit, the πνεῦμα,
not our little spirit and spiritualness, but God's spirit
triumphs, and that not in *his* pure spiritualness, but:
ἐγείρεται σῶμα πνευματικόν—the end of the ways of God
is corporealness. In this definition, the idea of God
with which Paul is truly concerned, appears in its un-
ambiguous superiority and critical intensity, dark

with final judgment and bright with highest hope. To misunderstand or misconstrue it would be ἀγνωσία θεοῦ.

One who has been able to follow our analysis of the book on the resurrection will understand these sentences. They contain a sweeping criticism of the usual conceptions of God. On what basis such a criticism can be made is not *clearly* seen. Only one fact is quite plain: Barth is struggling with all his might to realize God. His chief concern is to show that, if God is God, he must directly confront every one of us, so that something revolutionary will occur in our lives. He is convinced that Paul had come to this point and that he lived his life under the actuality of the total Otherness as it had revealed itself to him in Jesus Christ. The goal and purpose of Barth's commentaries on Paul's letters is, therefore, the recapturing of this apostolic quality of life. There can be no doubt that in the interpretation of I Cor., Barth successfully describes the decisiveness of Paul's faith in God. Naturally, such a description cannot have perfect definiteness, particularly since it is born of a profound restless seeking. Barth seems to raise more questions than he answers: from every answer that he gives several new questions seem to spring forth. He himself would be the last to deny this. From the very beginning of his "prophetic" career, he maintained that his writings should be regarded as a "marginal note" to *all* theology.

He probably never foresaw that this "marginal note" would contain such significant observations that books would have to be written to explain and defend it, and that a "theology" would eventually be developed from it. He was certain nevertheless that the note, merely as a note, was of gravest importance.

It was intended to remind the theologians and people in general that in their Christian faith they were confronted by *God*, that they were not dealing with the human as the human, but with the *human in its relation with God*. It was to call attention to the fact that the Bible (at least the New Testament) is not speaking of God in the impersonal manner of philosophers or metaphysicians whose thoughts about God are unrelated to practical issues of living, but in a manner that involves a radical change in the basic attitude and quality of existence, because God is *reality, ultimate* reality, from which there is no escape. He is not an *idea* or a *concept,* which one can hold or discard at pleasure.

Barth chose to make this "marginal note" in the form of commentaries. But shortly more than this was demanded of him. He had become the leader of a theological movement. Although his was not the only "voice crying in the wilderness," it was *he* who had felt the obligation "to prepare the way of the Lord," and he *had* to develop what he had once begun. He was expected to say more than could be said even in voluminous commentaries. He had to go the whole way—and the result was the "Barthian theology."

In the Preface to the fifth edition of the *Commentary on the Romans,* Barth states that he has been baffled by this development of things. He says: [4] "It may be that . . . in this book . . . something is pointed out which . . . the church and the theology of our time *had* to hear, to which they *had* to orient themselves. . . What shall I say, if here, perhaps without my willing it and in spite of me, as it were, something true, right and necessary has come to light, for the pure continuation and deepening execution of which I am made responsible as one of those who blew the horn at the decisive moment . . . I can only say to this, that, when I was writing the book in the remote peace of my Aargau parsonage, I had the feeling, characteristic of probably every eager author, of proposing something right and significant, but I had no idea that the consequences would be so great, that the Apostle Paul as I heard him would win such a response, that, with this book, I would encourage so many earnest men to question me, and drive me into a corner for further corrections, consequences, and even repetitions of what had already been brought to light. As if I were the man ordained for that! Admiral Tirpitz writes in his memoirs that it is easy to hoist the flag but difficult to haul it down with honor. I add: and it is still more difficult since the hauling down of the flag is out of the question—to keep it flying with honor. This is my situation. I have often wished, since writing this book, and having had to make up my mind on a subsequent program to follow, that I had never written it."

If we want to know how Barth kept his flag flying with honor, how he related his discoveries to the total content of Christian theology, how he transformed the marginal note into a "theology," we must return to the situation which made him write the books which we have just analysed. We must return to the pastorate and its problems. For the Barthian theology, as it is taking shape, is a practical, ecclesiastical theology, a science which is concerned with the message of the church, and with the sermon of the pastor in particular, as it is in the sermon that the ecclesiastical message finds expression.

The first volume of the *Dogmatics*, which has already appeared, explains the character of true theology, as Barth understands it. Before we discuss the importance of this work and its place in the general development of Barthian thought, we must first examine an address, delivered in October, 1922, entitled "The Word of God and the Task of the Ministry." An analysis of this lecture will help us to appreciate the real significance of his dogmatic theories. For here Barth has formulated in a few thetic sentences the principles of the theology upon which he is engaged at the present time.

These are his words: [5] "As ministers we ought to speak of God. We are human, however, and so cannot speak of God. We ought, therefore, to recognize both our obligation and our inability, and by that very recognition give God the glory." How must this statement be interpreted?

What does he mean when he says that the ministers ought to speak about God? On the basis of our analysis of his commentaries we can easily follow him when he addresses his fellow ministers: [6]

"Within the sphere of their own abilities and possibilities, the people are tolerably well adjusted; the reason that they come to us for wisdom, strange as it may seem, is because they know the whole network of their life is hung upon a thread like gossamer. They have suddenly awakened to a realization that they are walking upon a ridge between *time* and *eternity* that is narrower than a knife-edge. The theological problem comes into being at the *boundary* of mortality. The philosophers know this, but theologians many times seem not to.

"Obviously the people have *no* real need of *our* observations upon morality and culture, or even of our disquisitions upon religion, worship and the pos-

sible existence of other worlds. . . We may possibly
be able to give pleasure or help to this man or that,
or perhaps even to hundreds, by our more or less
stimulating preaching and satisfying teaching in regard to these troublesome questions. . . But let us
not think that by doing so we face the question
which really brings the people to us, or that we dis-
charge our duty as ministers of the Gospel by making adroit answers, or otherwise performing useful
ministries (religious ministries included) on *this*
level. . . When they come to us for help they do not
really want to learn more about *living*, they want
to learn more about what is on the farther edge of
living—*God*. We cut a ridiculous figure as village
sages or city sages. As such we are socially superfluous. We do not understand the profession of the
ministry unless we understand it as an index, a symp-
tom, say rather an omen, of a perplexity which ex-
tends over the whole range of human endeavor,
present and future. It is a perplexity felt by man
simply by virtue of his being a man, and has nothing
to do with his being moral *or* immoral, spiritual *or*
wordly, godly *or* ungodly. However conscious or
unconscious of his situation he may be, man cannot
escape his humanity, and humanity means limitation, finitude, creaturehood, separation from
God. . .

"Man as man cries for God. He cries not for a
truth, but for *truth*; not for something good, but
for *the* good; not for answers but for *the* answer. . .
He does not cry for solutions, but for salvation; not
for something human, but for God, for God as his
saviour from humanity. . . This answer, this subject, this meaning, this end, this reality, is never quite

here. The answer we may give is not also its own question; by it *here* and *beyond* are not merged in one. And yet when people ask for God, they do ask for an answer which is identical with their question. . . for one who is *beyond* and also *here,* for a God who is also *man."*

In other words: People come to church, because they desire an answer to the question regarding the meaning of life. To say that the meaning of life is living, to advise how living can be made rich and satisfying, to describe the path toward happiness, to explain that life is an infinite process and that the finest conscious life is one that is adjusted to the infinitude of the universe, to the profundities of its single factors as well as to its vast totality,—all this would not answer the question as to the meaning of life. The riddle is not, *how* live, but *why* live. Of course, one may laugh at the problem and exclaim: "I live and enjoy life." This is the attitude that men usually take. Or, on the other hand, one may become profoundly depressed and arrive at the conclusion that the problem is insoluble and that, therefore, life is meaningless—and nothing is left but to commit suicide. This, too, has been done, and is being done. These two ways illustrate the dilemma in which man finds himself. He is right in living the life that he has. But must he not, one day, awaken to the realization that he cannot live forever? He is right in accepting the fact of death. But is he also right in taking his own life, ending it before he has run his course? Man must live and he must die. The only possible way of finding an answer to the question as to the meaning of human existence is then to correlate life and death. Our existence would have a meaning if life and death no longer contradicted each other, if

we understood that life is death and death, life. But
as long as we are men, we cannot dissolve or overcome
this contradiction. We cannot, therefore, by ourselves,
answer the question. The only way out of our dilemma
is to receive an answer from beyond ourselves. If
another informs us that life has a meaning, we believe
him only if he has authority. If he tells us that we
ought to live or that we *ought* to die, we accept his
word only if he has behind him not the authority of
his own opinion or his own purpose, but an authority
which he too would obey. It is the "Wholly Other" to
which alone we can attribute *absolute* authority.
Everything within time is limited, just as we are, involved in the infinite contradiction between life and
death; the eternal alone is absolute. This "Wholly
Other," "Eternal," "Absolute" we call God. From
him alone, life can receive meaning. *He* gives life and
he takes it away: in him we know that we *ought* to
live and that, when the hour comes, we *ought* to die.
To live in him would mean death to an existence
which *we* controlled and determined; to die in him
would mean the overcoming of the meaninglessness
of death as the mere termination of existence.

If we could believe in this God, our life would have
a meaning, our question would be answered. But since
we cannot derive that faith from something within
ourselves—for everything human is in question—we
must receive it from beyond ourselves and from beyond the human. This is the reason we go to church,
and listen to the sermon, hoping to hear therein God's
authority. The human word of the minister is to convey to us the Word of God.

"We are human, however, and so cannot speak
of God." [7] "Our ministerial task is to say that *God*

becomes *man*, but say it as *God's* word, as God *himself* says it. This would be the answer to the question put to us by frightened consciences. This would
be the answer to man's question about redemption
from humanity. And it is this answer that should
be sounded as with a trumpet in our churches and
our lecture halls, and upon the streets, where the
men of our time are waiting to have us teach them
—but not as the scribes. The very reason we occupy
our pulpits and our professorial chairs is to say *this*
to them. . . The only answer that possesses genuine
transcendence, and so can solve the riddle of immanence, is God's word, note *God's* word."

Barth distinguishes three ways of giving this answer, of preaching God's word. The first way is *dogmatism.*

"When the minister is given the insight to realize
that the theme of the ministry is not man becoming
God but God becoming man—even when this insight flashes only occasionally upon his mind—he
acquires a taste for objectivity. . . He finds a world
which previously he had despised and hated as supernaturalism slowly but surely becoming reasonable
and purposeful. He understands it, so to speak, from
within, from behind.

"But obviously one cannot speak of God even in
the most powerfully and vividly conceived supernaturalism. . . The weakness of orthodoxy is not the
supernaturalistic element in the Bible and the dogmas; on the contrary in that lies its strength. It is
rather the fact that orthodoxy, and we all, so far
as we are in our own way dogmaticians, have a way
of regarding some objective description of that element—such as the word "God" for instance—as the

element itself. . . By this kind of answer a man's question about God is simply quashed. He no longer has a question. In place of the question, he has an answer. But as long as he remains a man, he cannot let the question go. . . Any answer would have to assume his nature and become itself a question. To hold the word "God" or anything else before a man with the demand that he believe it, is not to speak of God. The fact is that a man cannot believe what is simply held *before* him. He can believe nothing that is not both *within* him and before him. He *cannot* believe what does not *reveal* itself to him, that has not the power to penetrate to him. God by himself is not God. He might be something else. Only the God who reveals himself that is God. The God who becomes man is God. But the dogmatist does not speak of this God."

The second way is *self-criticism* or *mysticism*.

"On this way any man who desires to have a part in God is bidden as a man to die, to surrender all his uniqueness, his self-hood, his ego-hood, and to be still, unassuming, direct. . . God is not this or that; he is no object, no something, no opposite, no second; he is pure being, without quality, filling everything, obstructed only by the particular individuality of man. Let this latter finally be removed and the soul will of certainty conceive God.

"The mystic knows that man really desires One who is *not himself*. I call this the way of self-criticism—though it may also be understood as the way of idealism—because by it a man places himself under judgment and negatives himself, because it shows so clearly that what must be overcome is man as man.

"But even here we cannot speak of God. The mystics, and we all in so far as we are mystics, have been wont to *assert* that what annihilates and enters into man, the abyss into which he falls, . . . the No before which he stands, is *God*; but this we are incapable of *proving*. . . . . But let us remember that no self-negation to which we may refer men (were it even suicide), is so great and so profound as the actuality, as the self-negation which is immediately imbued with the positivity of God. The keener the criticism of man, the more keenly man's question is emphasized as a question. But this is only to indicate correctly—how God must be spoken of *if* man is denied. It is not however to speak of God. . . . *God* has not become man. *Man* has become man with a vengeance, but there is no salvation in that."

Neither the appeal to external authority nor to the pure voice within will enable the minister to speak with absolute certainty. Supernaturalism and dogmatism are forms of speaking of God which never bring him into a relationship with man. The dogmatist can never show how his God can become a God *for* man. The method of mysticism is equally inadequate. It criticizes the human as the non-divine, assuming, after the extinction of the human, that it will experience the rise of a God-consciousness; but as a matter of fact it is never God who speaks in the "emptiness" of the mystic's heart—it is always still the human. The modern psychological approach to a knowledge of God is not as different from mysticism as it may seem. Mysticism speaks of *man* under the aspect of self-criticism; modernism deals with him under the aspect of self-assertion. The mystic believes that God will reveal himself in the human soul, after it has been negativated; the modernist also finds God in the human soul, but in its highest and purest positive expressions of thought, will and emotion. But both the mystic *and* the modernist speak of *man* and *not* of *God*.

The true way of speaking about God would be to combine the methods of the dogmatist *and* the mystic. Justice must be done to the "Otherness" of God as well as to the longing of the human heart to have God as its own. This way is that of *dialectic*.[8]

It "undertakes . . . to develop the idea of God on the one hand, and the criticism of man and all things human on the other; but they are not now considered independently, but are both referred to their common presupposition, to the living truth, which to be sure may not be named, but which lies between them and gives to both their meaning and interpretation. Here there is an unwavering insight into the fact that the living truth, the determining content of any real utterance concerning God, is that God (but really God!) becomes man (but really man!).

"But how now shall the necessary dependence of both sides of the truth upon this living Center be established? The genuine dialectician knows that this Center cannot be apprehended or beheld, and he will not, if he can help it, allow himself to be drawn into giving direct information about it, knowing that *all* such information, whether it be positive or negative, is *not* really information, but always *either* dogma *or* self-criticism. On this narrow ridge of rock one can only walk: if he attempts to stand still, he will fall either to the right or to the left, but fall he must. There remains only to keep walking—an appalling performance for those who are not free from dizziness—looking *from one side to the other,* from positive to negative and from negative to positive."

This is the earliest description of the *dialectical method* that we can find in Barth's writings. From it, his theology received the name, "dialectical theology." With the help of this method he commenced to construct his own system. He has obviously designed it to avoid the mistake of the dogmatist, who is liable to assert his theological convictions in scholastic formalism and meaningless doctrinairism. He also avoids the errors of the mystic or of the modernist. The theology of the first is often intelligible only to one versed in psycho-pathology, and that of the latter often frankly appears as atheistic humanism. What, then, is the dialectical method? It does not directly assert God, because man can never assume the place of God and speak in his stead. Nor does it propose to present a form of atheism or religious agnosticism on the ground that all that man can ever say of the highest, of the most truly divine itself, remains a human expression, and a *human* opinion or idea. It is both atheistic *and* dogmatic, negative *and* positive. It presupposes that an irrational supernaturalism or authoritarianism *as well as* a radical, frank atheism are preferable to any form of theological rationalism which attempts to understand the reality of God by reasoning process. It presupposes that God is not man, that God as God is beyond the human realm.

Does the dialectician lead, then, to certainty concerning God? No, he does not. His method is not a means toward such an end. It is rather the expression of that attitude of mind which is the result of the belief that life is meaningful only if it is related to the "Wholly Other," the "Yonder," the "Origin," God. The dialectical method is one of description. It depicts *man* in his relation with *God*. It deals with human life as it is influenced by the crisis which develops from the realization of death, by the crisis which becomes apparent in the question as to the meaning of life. The dialectician does not speak of God in the affirmative way of the dogmatist, nor in the negative way of the mystic, nor in the rationalistic way of the modernist critic. *Setting aside all these methods, he makes room for God himself to speak.*

When the quest for the meaning of life awakens in a man, he has forebodings that only the authority, the *revelation* of a "Wholly Other" can answer. He can no longer continue to live under the naïve assumption that his harmless, self-sufficient existence prior to the appearance of the crisis, was the good life. He has come to consider it an illusion. He does not try to replace this dream by another in the assertion of having apprehended and therefore possessing that "Yonder" which caused his disillusionment. He will rather live in constant awareness of that which is "beyond," knowing there is an answer though as yet unreceived. The psychoanalysts are quite familiar with the attitude which we are here describing. They try to educate their patients to that sense of objectivity which will disillusion them and teach them to shape their lives according to this sense. When they attempt to describe ultimate objectivity as it is reflected in the perfectly "adjusted" life, they have to resort to the dialectical method. In order to make plain what constitutes ultimate objectivity, they have to use both positive *and* negative terms.

When Barth defines the dialectical method, he makes Christian faith its keystone. The Christian believes that the "Wholly Other," which constitutes ultimate objectivity, has *revealed* itself in Jesus Christ. Such, Barth maintains, was the faith of Paul and the Apostles. They believed, he says, that God *had* revealed himself, and in their messages, testified to this revelation. Believing in the *Lord* Jesus Christ, they spoke of God's revelation in him; but in speaking of God, they spoke dialectically. They were bearing witness *to* the revelation, but, in describing the revelation, they did not affirmatively declare what it was, but spoke of it in the dialectical way, both in the positive *and* in the negative manner. They spoke of God in terms which did not deprive him of his ultra-human otherness nor themselves of his presence. Believing, to them, did not mean seeing God, but having the "spirit" of God. The divine to them was distinctly transcendent, but this conception did not prevent them from joyfully proclaiming its immanence in the believer. One great assumption, however, underlay all this, their belief, namely, that God himself had really spoken, that he had disclosed himself in him whom they called "Lord." Jesus Christ, a name which designates in a *dialectical* way the togetherness of God *and* man, was in their belief the *"word"* of God. All those who share, or desire to share, this faith, must follow the early Christians in this dialectical theology, a "Theology of the Word."

Such is the character of Barthian theology as it stands today. What we have explained in the last paragraphs is the theme of the last books and publications of Karl Barth, particularly of his *Dogmatik*, the first volume of which appeared under the title: "The Doc-

trine of the Word of God." But the commentary on
Paul's Epistle to the Philippians, the second volume of
collected essays, entitled "Theology and the Church,"
and the most recent articles, particularly one on "The
Doctrine of the Holy Spirit," belong to this last phase
of Barthian thought.

One more word should be said about the "Dogmatics," for this work shows Barth in an entirely new
light. It differs widely from his earlier books, especially the *Commentary on the Romans*. Even the style
has changed. To be sure, it has lost none of its force-
fulness and of its fluency in expressing the most deli-
cate and involved theological ideas; but the almost
bewildering use of paradoxical terms has disappeared.
The passion of the prophet who presents his conviction by attacking the whole theological and intellectual world, tearing it to pieces with the fire, sword
and thunder of inspiration, has become the quest of
the scholar who, as calmly as his subject will permit,
presents his arguments, with persuasive and appealing
eagerness pointing to the truth as he sees it, and with
merciless and incisive thoroughness dissecting the
theories and opinions of those whom he criticizes.
Barth reveals here astonishing constructive ability.
Following a remarkably clear and consistent outline,
he presents his system as one unity, leading from one
thesis to another. Furthermore, he discloses tremendous industry. While at the outset of his career as an
author, he spoke as an exceedingly well educated and
informed theologian, today he displays, in the frequent references to the works of the great theological
teachers of the church universal, an extraordinarily
broad knowledge of theological literature. He gives us
the impression that he has labored for the elucidation

of truth with the thoroughness which befits a true teacher and scholar. He does not speak like a man who, at any cost, must stand by a once uttered conviction, but like one who is working to establish truth because it has overwhelmed him. While there are hardly any direct statements in his writings that he has given thought to the numerous criticisms that have been leveled against him, there is plenty of indirect evidence that he has. The terminology especially has been refined with great care, and the fundamental arguments are introduced as comprehensively as possible. Nobody may, therefore, light-heartedly turn away from him. Everyone who is concerned about the same problem as Barth, *must* pay attention to him.

It is well here to summarize the result of the survey of Barth's theological development, though such an undertaking is obviously very difficult, because of the need to label or classify this "system."

An attempt might be made to look for Barth's theological ancestors. It has often been pointed out by the critics of Barthianism that the whole movement is a revival of Calvinism. Barth himself refers to his Reformed heritage and considers himself particularly responsible for the future of that group within Protestantism which owes its existence to the work of Calvin. But significant as this connection is —and it is doubtless very significant—it reveals nothing definite, for he cites the authority of Luther just as often as he does that of the Genevan reformer, and could, on this account, as well be called a Lutheran. Should one see then in Barthianism a revival of the theology and the religion of the Reformation? That would be correct in the sense that Barth

and his friends, without question, maintain that the
reformers understood the meaning of Christianity
better than any of the theologians since Schleiermacher. But they would certainly object if their
theology were said to be a *return* to the Reformation.
They stand *in principle* for the same cause as Luther,
Calvin, and the Reformation. But that is about all
that can be affirmed in this connection.

What is this cause and what is this principle? Is it
Biblicism? Yes, but the authority of the Scripture
which they teach is surely not the same as that which
Calvin made the basis of his Institutes. It is not the
Book of the Bible nor the Biblical word which Barth
desires to recover as an authoritative norm, but the
"Word" in the words of the Bible. It is a principle
which becomes apparent in the writings of Paul—as
also in the prophetic sayings of Jeremiah: the principle of divine righteousness. If Barth has a line of
theological ancestors, it includes all those who have
taught that God is not man and that in this life man
must be constantly aware of the presence of the
divine "Otherness." In other words, Barth defends the
validity of the idea of revelation—not a certain *concept* of it, but the idea which is *meant* by the *religious*
term "revelation."

We are now in a position to characterize more
specifically this theology, particularly if we keep in
mind the historical analysis given in the second chapter of this book. Barth is interested in the Christian
religion in so far as it is the belief that God has revealed himself in Jesus Christ. All his writings are
devoted to showing what this belief can *mean* to the
man of the Twentieth Century. Since he is convinced
that the modern church has lost the meaning of its

message, he opposes it with all the enthusiasm which marks a religious prophet who is persuaded of the truth of his teachings.

The peculiar complexity of Barth's thought is due to the fact that he in no way denies the distinctive tasks which the church of today must fulfill. He is not a conservative who closes his eyes to the necessities of a new era. He does not try to stem the course of modern life as it is influenced by scientific research in all fields of knowledge and enterprise. He does not reject the findings of historical criticism in theology and in the church. He is *thoroughly* contemporaneous in every way. And yet he claims that the faith of Paul must and can be ours.

But, with all this, we have not yet called attention to the most significant issue of Barth's thought. It will become clear when we ask: What are the *reasons* for his rebellion against the modern church? One might be inclined to answer as follows. He entered the Christian ministry as a religious individualist imbued with the liberal Christian theology of W. Herrmann, but was not yet certain of himself. His early articles indicate that he made certain mental reservations. His inner restlessness became apparent when he joined the group around Kutter and the religious Socialists, attacking the social and economic structure of the modern world in the name of conscience. Under the influence of the war, he lost faith in the methods of the Socialists, and began to despair of the possibility of reforming modern civilization. Having lost all confidence in himself as well as in his world, he began to look for a certainty beyond himself. He was thus led to re-assert the authority of that part of the Christian tradition which emphasizes the other-worldly sovereignty of God under the principle, *Deo gloria.* His theology is, therefore, the expression of a feeling, more or less common in post-war Europe and especially in Germany, arising from the realization of a general bankruptcy of civilization.

Such a description of the Barthian theology has often been given, particularly by those who would like to dismiss it because it is uncomfortable, but, it really does not explain it at its most vital point. Our general review of the writings of Barth must have revealed that he is primarily concerned with an understanding of life. His theology has grown out of the desire to face life honestly in its height and depth. It is not a defense of Christian tradition and an attack upon modernism for the sake of Christian tradition. It does not represent a reaction against the cultural optimism of liberal Protestantism on the basis of post-war disappointment and for the sake of a return into the safe otherworldliness of God. It is the expression of man's chief interest, his quest for the meaning of life. This theology is, therefore, thoroughly *human.* Orthodox and liberal Christianity, pre- and post-war conditions, the Bible and even God are significant only in so far as they have their place in *the* human question and its answer. The only premise which is necessary for the understanding of the Barthian theology is the admission of the fact that human existence is problematical, mysterious. On this basis Barth presents his teachings. His message is that one can live meaningfully and truthfully only by the faith that God, the "Wholly Other," has revealed himself in Jesus Christ.

This message, however, is not as simply explained as it is stated. It involves numerous theological problems.

In the succeeding chapters, we shall discuss them in detail. They may here he stated as follows:

The first and outstanding element in Barth's teaching is his *anti-subjectivism* or the *radical breach with the tradition of liberal theology since Kant and Schleiermacher*. As we pointed out in one of the preceding chapters, the character of this theology was determined by its recognition of the place that reason holds in the understanding of life. Since it had to accept the world-view developed by the sciences, and particularly by the natural sciences which had sprung up in connection with and in consequence of the emancipation of reason, it had to assert and explain the contents of religious knowledge, especially man's belief in God, in accord with this world-view and in terms which would be in harmony with the principles of modern philosophy. The theologians and philosophers of the Enlightenment were losing the particular and historical character of the positive religions by making religion a part of a general rationalism. In contrast to them, Schleiermacher established the principles of modern theology, which seemingly enabled it to do justice to the unique essence of religious belief and particularly of the Christian faith. He described religion as a certain attitude of the human soul; and he viewed historical religions in their historical character, dating them back to their founders. In the principles of Psychologism and Historism he seemed to have discovered means by which the peculiar knowledge of religion could be explained without violating the philosophical and scientific principles of reason. Since that time systems of theology have been developed which depend on the various types of modern philosophy, from Idealism to Pragmatism, according to the philosophical traits and preferences of the individual theologians; and they have been based on interpretations of religious experiences, both of the present and of the past. The questions: what is the essence of religious experience, what is the character of Christian experience, in which way can or must faith depend on history? have been paramount in theology. This type of theology has resulted in the loss of the belief in the absoluteness of Christianity and in the unique character of the Christian's knowledge of God. Religious individualism or subjectivism and historical relativism, the two principles which according to Barth in his early writings, constitute modern theology, can give no guarantee of absolute truth.

So far we have not stated the most radical and revolutionary consequence of modern theology: the loss of the "realism of faith." By realism of faith we mean the certainty of the existence of God which in the pre-rationalistic era was held without serious difficulty since it accorded with many world-views as well as philosophies. Modern philosophy and science allow only a concept of God. How can theology then assert and explain the reality of God on which religion depends if it is to be more than a philosophical attitude—since it has always claimed it to be more!

The outstanding feature of the theology of Karl Barth can now be stated: he wants to return to this religious realism. In contrast to the subjectivism of modern theology, he preaches the reality, the objectivity of God. It must always be kept in mind that Barthianism is a theology of contrast, of *this* contrast. Herein lies its tremendous power. It gives expression to the general feeling that modern theology does *not* speak with authority.

To some it may seem as if Barth had joined the ranks of those traditionalists who have persistently refused to accept the modern world-view in order to preserve the old religious realism, but as a matter of fact, Barth is no "fundamentalist."

The second element of Barthianism is *Biblicism.* It is linked in a curious way with what we described in the preceding paragraph. For Barth discovered "Christian realism" in the Bible and in Paul's letters in particular. The significant fact about this discovery is that he made it not as an academic theologian, but as a preacher and pastor. It is important to remember in this connection that the difference between modern preaching in America and Protestant Europe is fundamental. The American sermon is seldom Biblical and expository. Its reference to the Scripture is in the majority of cases casual or superficial. It deals generally with "religious" topics. The European Protestant, however, follows the old tradition of preaching the "Word," whether he is affiliated with liberal or orthodox theology. To the preacher Barth, the exposition of the "Word" was a particularly pressing and grave problem. When he finally found a solution, he discovered in the Bible that "realism" which modern theology could not convey.

The third element of Barthianism, is that he felt that the Bible must be interpreted in an entirely new way. His conviction of the reality of God, which was nourished and upheld by his new understanding of the Bible, was identical with the belief that, as God, God was not man, but the "Totally Other." The Biblical phrase which had engaged his attention very early in his theological career, that God lives in a light no man can approach unto, now revealed itself to him in its full meaning. From man's point of view, God is the unknowable and unapproachable. If man is to know him, he can do so not through his *own* efforts or experiences, but only by the accepting of God's revelation, in which God discloses himself as the subject of faith. He has ceased to be merely the object of pious religious devotion.

Two features of Barth's Biblicism are, therefore, outstanding: One is that he believes that the men of the Bible have recognized the total "Otherness" of God in pointing to the *revelation* which occurred in Jesus Christ. The Christian message can consequently be understood only as a testimony to the belief that the otherwise unknowable God has disclosed himself to the believing mind in Jesus Christ. What this revelation is, since it is not considered miraculously supernatural nor identified with the historical Jesus, as we have pointed out before, must be explained in another connection.

The other feature is that the only method and means by which this testimony of God's revelation can be given, according to Barth, is the *dialectical method,* which refrains from stating it in either positive or negative terms while *pointing* out the absolute truth that the world of God is totally different from the world of man. No word of man, therefore, can be the word of God unless it is dialectically broken in the remembrance of the "infinite qualitative difference between time and eternity."

The fourth element of Barthianism is a *new anthropology.* In discussing Barth's theological development it has been brought out that his theology was connected with a very specific and unique view of human

life, that it was based on an analysis of human existence, characterized by the unescapable fact of death.

The principles of Barthianism may be analyzed as
the following:

1. What is the meaning of the Realism of God?

2. Of what kind is the authority of the Biblical
word?

3. What is the character of the divine revelation in
Jesus Christ?

4. What is the dialectical method?

5. In what way are these doctrines founded upon a
new anthropology?

V

BARTH'S CONCEPTION OF CHRISTIANITY

IT is now possible to proceed with a more complete analysis of these various aspects of the Barthian theology. In the preceding chapter, a picture has been presented showing its development and its themes, but we have not yet reached an understanding of Christianity as Barth thinks of it both in a critical and a constructive way.

Our next task is, therefore, to describe in detail Barth's picture of Christianity. First we shall discuss the *Commentary on the Romans,* and then the "Dogmatics." In these discussions we must constantly keep in mind the results of the analyses of the last chapter.

In order to understand Barth's view of Christianity, it is necessary first to consider his concept of the problematical character of life. At this point American Christians and theologians will experience their chief difficulty in following him, for his views are nearly the opposite of theirs. If one looks at human life from the point of view of progressive evolution, he must of necessity be unresponsive to Barth's plea. If one holds the opinion that the universe which has produced such a remarkable being as man, is good and friendly, and that one must, therefore, trust in the total life-process; if he identifies religion with "cosmic emotion" and finds God in the cosmos and regards man as its final product; and if, in consequence of all this, he holds an optimistic outlook on life, confident that all its difficulties can or will be overcome in wise adjustment to the order of the universe, he cannot fail to stand aghast at the totally contrary judgment of Barth.

"Whence comes," he asks [1], "this strange longing of modern man to see glaciers, the desert, the North Pole, the unfathomable ocean, and the wayless realms of the air, that which is infinitely small, the gruesome events of the millions of years through which nature has passed, the petty miseries of his own history, the absurdities which according to the testimony of trustworthy experts occur in the subconscious and occult morass of his own existence—what is this desire for the experience and the knowledge of a thousand things, such as an unbroken man who lives spontaneously certainly would not wish to experience or to know? And why is it that the experience of the cosmos as it becomes more thorough and more complete refuses to minimize the problematical character of human life, but rather increases it more and more?" Man seeks rest in the cosmos that is *his own* and everywhere he encounters *his own* restlessness. The universe with its contrasts of war and peace, life and death, finiteness and infinity reflect the conflict of human existence.

Our life is perplexing. Its limitations, its constant relativity, its ups and downs from pain to joy, its doubts of a supreme good, especially its continuous standing face to face with active evil, enclose us within a wall we cannot surmount; they throw us back into the restlessness and sufferings of life. We are creatures, and we suffer from our creaturehood in unspeakable pain. We can never live as if we were the masters of our fate. We are given over to the unceasing movements of force and matter, of growing up and withering away, of the desire to live and the necessity of dying. The joy of living inspired by the animalistic instinct which the Greeks called Eros is forever broken by the reality of death. The genius and even the prophet await the same fate as the microbe. How can such a life be spontaneously real and true? The world is unredeemed.

There is nothing in life which is not determined by the inevitable necessity of death. "My hunger and my need for sleep, my sexuality and the fight for my existence, my temperament and my originality, my insatiable desire for knowledge, the play of my artistic feelings, the storms of my will and finally my religious need, together with the corresponding macrocosmic and social instincts—they are all rooted in the temporary, accidental, perishable complexity of my body; they all constitute a life which is surrendered to death." [2] Death indeed seems to be the highest law of this world. Everything which tends toward a renewal of life appears only in characteristic form of destruction: morality demands often a negation of the body in the name of the spirit; philosophy discovers its true essence and tendency in the figure of the dying Socrates; progress can take place only in restless negation of what is existent; the flame burns only if it consumes.

Human life is characterized by a profound restlessness. Nowhere is there peace, nowhere certainty, nowhere security. Man lives and he must die. He recognizes truths, purposes, meanings, but the more he knows, the less he can say about truth and purpose and meaning. He knows the good that should happen, what he ought to do; but the greater his knowledge of the good, the surer he is that he will not, that he cannot do it. He dreams a dream of his God-likeness, and opens his eyes to discover that he is standing on a middle ground between angel and animal; it is this he calls humanity. He thinks the final, ultimate thought of God, of eternity, of the absolute, and in thinking notices that he has conceived only a thing, a time, something relative, enormously relative. Nowhere can he settle down; he must always march on. He is *homo viator*, always on his way.[3]

Relativism is here seriously affirmed in its radical aspects. The puzzling perplexity of life, which is only too shockingly revealed to us every morning when we look into the newspaper; its problematical, questionable, certainly never absolute qualities which are there disclosed to us in baffling banality—all this Barth faces with dispassionate, coolest impartiality. He has been called an archpessimist, who persistently refuses to see the good, promising sides of the human endeavor. He is said to have stubbornly overlooked the sincere and certainly not hopeless efforts of men to build an orderly existence, to live peaceably with each other, to conform to the necessities which are presented to us by the universe of which we are a part. As a matter of fact, Barth would never fail to admit that all these things are worthy and good. He would never hesitate to join in any campaign against evil, whatever and wherever it might be. He would never question the necessity to fight famines and pestilences, oppressions and wars, to extinguish fear and to combat superstition. The one reservation, however, that he would make most decisively, before identifying himself with such undertakings, would be the warning against the expectation that by such means the ceaseless quest for the good life could be silenced, that the attainment of any of such goals or of all of them would be equal to an attainment of God.

He is a pessimist only in so far as he feels compelled to disparage any view of life which is not definitely based upon the recognition of its relative, finite, problematical, unredeemed nature. In his eyes, any *human* answer to the *question* of the meaning of life, any human statement of what is true, good, absolute, is superstitious, utopian, illusory. The *question* and the *crisis* which we suffer because of it, cannot and must never be given up. For "in the *question* of its meaning we must recognize the last, definitely *last* meaning of our temporal existence." And in recognizing this, "we think, under profoundest emotion, of the idea 'eternity.' The deepest '*Problem*' of our existence is, therefore, also its deepest truth." [4]

We here touch again the heart of all Barthian thinking: the *crisis* of all that is in time points to the *eternal*; the questionability, the relativity of things existent, points to the answering, absolute *origin*; the limited creaturehood of the world and what is in it, points to the *Creator*. It is the qualitative difference between time and eternity which is referred to here. It is the Neo-Kantian idea of the "origin," also already mentioned, which is here given theological significance by being practically identified with the attitude of the man of the Bible toward God. "For every philosophy which understands itself is, as is also the Biblical, transcendental thinking—*i.e.*, it does not stop with certain material principles or with something that is given physically or psychologically; it ends where the most primitive and the most advanced meditations of the human mind inevitably end: it points to that relation in which everything given stands toward a last something that is *not* given: it ends with the recognition of an origin. All philosophy that understands itself, from Plato to Kant, is transcendental philosophy, philosophy of origin and not philosophy of immanence or of ideality. Recognition of the origin or God's relation with man is the one theme around which both Biblical and philosophical thinking center." [5]

The understanding of the theology of crisis stands and falls with the true understanding of this main theme. One may see in it first of all the expression of a profound scepticism, a scepticism, to be sure, not as to a "that," but as to the "what." The word "origin," the infinite qualitative difference between God and man, may mean *that* God is the ultimate reality, but that it is impossible to say *what* this reality is. God is never a reality of life. If he were that, he would not be God but an idol; and as such he would be doubted and questioned, together with all things of this life and this world. The true God reveals himself just when these "realities" are found lacking and when they break down. His "reality" is disclosed in the crisis of human and earthly values. Whenever existence in time is drawn into question, whenever the meaning of human life is uncertain, God reveals himself. The scepticism of Barth, is therefore, finally directed against man, in so far as he claims to be or to have anything definite or absolute.

God alone, as the totally "Other," is the absolute. He is not a something among other things, not even a *Ding an sich* among others, not a higher being among

other beings, a highest unknown power among the
well-known physical or mental powers. He is the totally "Other" in so far as everything existent stands
in transcendental *relation* to him. He is, therefore, not
a cause—not even the first cause from which everything would be derived, since as such he would not be
the *Wholly Other*—and yet he does not represent a
metaphysical world of the Yonder which would be
radically isolated from the Here, and since as such his
relationship with this world would be nullified. God
is the totally "Other" because he is that which *constitutes* the restless questioning, the unredeemed limitation of this world. He is the answer which is sought
in all questions about the meaning of life—and as such
he must be "totally Other" than the question: he must
be its fulfillment, its end. He is that which limits and
is therefore totally other than limitation. But such a
question could not arise without the answer—and in
this case the answer is really primary to the question
("Thou wouldst not seek me hadst thou not already
found me," said Pascal) : limitation demands one or
something that limits.

Barth, it must be clearly understood does not teach
a metaphysical dualism. God is not a transcendent X,
outside of this world, existent in supreme isolation.
Whoever is unable to understand the *transcendental
relation* in which God is *related* with the world, will
never grasp the meaning of the Barthian theology. He
will almost inevitably fall into the error of describing it as a dualistic theology. In the words of Brunner:[6] when the theologians of crisis speak of the transcendent God, they are "treating of an epistemological
but not a cosmological transcendence." They revive
the old slogan of the Reformed Church, *Finitum non*

capax infiniti, which means that, from the viewpoint
of man, God is always the unknown, the remote. When
man speaks of God on the basis of human need, when
God becomes the tool for his use, when he is described
as the highest form or expression of human values or
ideals, as that which is supreme in the world as man
knows it, God appears as a human possibility, a creation of human purposes, an idol from the worship of
which one must awaken sooner or later to the realization that he has stood face to face not with God but
with man and the human world. Such worship is
tolerable only to one who is satisfied with his human
existence and sufficient unto himself. No one, however, who feels the crisis of today can find peace in
such an effort.

It means that religion itself, as it is commonly understood, is not a means of salvation. To be religious
can never be identical with having found God. Religion is usually nothing else than the desire to overcome the limitations of life; it is the passion for infinity, the longing for rest in the midst of restlessness.
As such it is doubtless the noblest expression of humanity, the climax of its dignity, but it is also the cul-
mination of its problematical, unredeemed nature and
character. True religion *points* to the "Yonder"
whence salvation may come, but it does not possess
or control this "Yonder." Even religion is part of the
world; it is the world in its psychological, intellectual,
moral and sociological form. Our religious consciousness never enables us to overcome our mortality; it
does not provide us with an escape from our own
selves as they are imbedded in the pains of the world.
It only *hints* at the totally "Other." Whenever religious experience claims to possess the absolute God,

whenever an institution built upon such an experience claims absolute authority for itself, the sin against the Holy Spirit is committed. The distance which separates man from God is then disregarded. Promethean Titanism is again guilty of *hybris*. Adam has again eaten the fruit which he, as *man*, is forbidden to taste. He has again listened to the seducer and believed his words: *"Eritis sicut Deus."* And when he comes to himself, he must discover that the burden of being a man is heavier than before.

It is the religious man, especially, who must come to the realization that God is in heaven and that he himself is on earth, that God, the real God, and man can never become one, that the fulness of God is out of his reach, that, even if he were a prophet and a religious genius, he could not take the place of God. To be a religious man means, therefore, to be a torn, inharmonious, peaceless man. Only the unreligious person—if there is one—who is indifferent to the question about God, can be in tune with himself and with the universe. All others must discover that the meaning of religion is death. There is then no longer room in religion for supremely beautiful and lovely feelings and for refinement of humanity. But in reality, here is abyss, here is horror. Here one sees demons (Ivan Karamazov and Luther!). *"Der altböse Feind ist unheimlich nahe."* "The reality of religion is struggle, sin and death, devil and hell; it shocks; it offends. It does not lead man out of his bewilderment as to guilt and fate, but rather into it. It does not give him a solution of his life-problem, but renders his existence insolubly puzzling. It is neither his redemption nor its discovery, but it is the uncovering of his longing for it. It cannot be enjoyed nor celebrated, but must be borne as a hard yoke which cannot be cast off. Religion cannot be recommended to anyone: it is a misfortune which with a fatal necessity descends upon certain people and by their activity and behavior befalls others also. It is the misfortune under the pressure of which John the Baptist went into the desert to preach repentance and judgment; under the pressure of which such a stirring, heavy sigh as the second letter to the Corinthians was written; under the gruesome pressure of which a physiognomy comes to look like that of the old Calvin. It is the misfortune under which probably every man is secretly suffering." [7]

In so far as religious experience is affirmed, it is understood to be that mood and inner attitude in which man becomes aware of his need of salvation, in which he opens his soul in readiness for the redemption which must come from without, because he cannot give it to himself. "I must give, risk, sacrifice everything, in order to attain the one necessity, the 'being like God' —and when I have risked everything, given everything, sacrificed everything, I must find that my hands are empty, that I am more estranged and more remote from the 'One' than before." [8] Man feels that in order to be saved he must know God, but inevitably he has to discover that as man he *cannot* know God. Religion *sees* the hills from whence cometh one's help, but *cannot carry* the human soul to them.

There is no way from man to God; no religious experience can overcome the borderline which separates the human from the divine. But what is impossible to man has been made possible by God himself: in Jesus Christ the reality of God has become apparent. In him God has revealed himself. In him the longing of man,

most profoundly expressed in his pious life, is fulfilled. In him *God* himself speaks to man.

But let no one think that in Jesus the eternal God
is directly accessible. Not the so-called historical Jesus
is the Christ, but he who was crucified and rose from
the dead. The cross and the resurrection—these make
Jesus the Christ. If his life is not seen in the light of
his death, God is not disclosed in him. "He goes as a
sinner among the sinners. He subjects himself to the
judgment under which the world stands. He places
himself where God can be present only as a question
about God. . . On the peak, at the end of his course,
he is a purely negative figure: certainly not a genius,
by no means the bearer of manifest or occult psychic
powers, surely not a hero, leader, poet or thinker; but
just in this negation (My God, my God, why hast thou
forsaken me!), just in the fact of his sacrificing all
the psychic, heroic, aesthetic possibilities of this genius
to an invisible "Other," is he the fulfillment of all
human development as it reaches its climax in the law
and the prophets, who were always pointing beyond
themselves. . . The Messiah is the *end* of man." [9] Jesus
the healer and physician, Jesus the prophet, Jesus the
Messiah, Jesus the Son of God must be seen in the light
of the crucified Jesus. All human possibilities are sus-
pended. Neither the personality nor the teachings of
Jesus disclose God, not even where they are *confirmed*
by his death on the cross. Those aspects of the life and
death of Jesus which are historically recognizable,
which, when added one to another, result in the picture of the so-called historical Jesus, the life and religion of the Jewish prophet Jesus of Nazareth, belong to the plane of the historical and psychological.
They are never the divine and the eternal. From a

human, historical point of view, his death can be understood only as a heroic sacrifice, in principle *no* different from the sacrifice of a mother for her child, of a soldier for his country, of a physician for the welfare of humanity. But as soon as this life, this death are seen in relation to the unknown, remote God, they are a divine revelation to us, a word of God to man. For *this* man, *this* prophet, *this* teacher, *this* hero, *this* performer of miracles is negated. He dies that the son of *God* may live. The death of Jesus is the disclosure of the relativity of all that is of this world; it is the suspension of all values of life. It is the end of man and what is best in him, and as such is the beginning of God. It is the revelation of the absolute "Otherness" of God, the disclosure of the last possibilities of divine wrath, the unfolding of the question of God in its sharpest and most unescapable sense.

The crucifixion, however, can thus be understood only in the light of the resurrection. Jesus, the crucified, is the Christ because he rose from the dead. Like Paul and like the reformers, Barth does not think of the cross aside from the resurrection. Only the risen Christ completes the revelation. He gives the assurance of the *mercy* of God. He reveals the divine "Yes." But let no one think of the resurrection as a historical event among the facts of this life. It is rather *the* unhistorical event, surrounding all events as their limitation, leaving the manifestation of the unknown God as such unrevealed, hinting only at the transcendent mercy of God. No continuity can exist between the story of the resurrection (*i.e.* the empty grave, or the occult appearances of the risen Lord in Jerusalem, or the visions as reported in I. Cor. 15), and the resurrection itself. For should it be in any sense a fact of our history or of time, it would also belong in the plane of the up and down of life and death. In the resurrection the new world, the world of God's original creation touches the universe as a tangent touches a circle. To believe in the resurrection of Jesus means to relate him to the unseen, unknown God.[10]

This Christology, which is by no means complete and leaves room for many questions, as Barth himself would have admitted after he had written his *Commentary on the Romans*—is in no way a new feature in Barth's thinking. It is in accordance with its principal theme: whenever the meaning of human life is uncertain, whenever the values of this world are drawn into question, God reveals himself as the "Totally Other," in the infinite qualitative difference between time and eternity. The *Deus revelatus* is the *Deus absconditus*.

The following problem arises at this point: Is Barth's Christology an illustration of his view of God and the world, or is his doctrine of God derived from the New Testament and its message of Jesus the Christ? Certain of his statements may lead us to assume that the second assumption is correct; for he affirms very definitely that although a foreshadowing of the truth can be found elsewhere than in the teachings of the New Testament, we know the truth only in Jesus Christ. "In his light we see the light." [11]

We should be aware, however, of the fact that Barth has to make one very significant presupposition in order to consider this interpretation of Jesus Christ the authority on which all theology must be based. His Christology, in a word, is developed on the ground of the assumption that God is and that he must be understood as the "Totally Other," whose supreme freedom and sovereignty will never permit him to be identified with values in the world of man. Only in the light of this doctrine of God, can Barth develop his Christology. Must we then come to the conclusion that all he has to say about Jesus Christ is nothing but a repetition of his own conception of God, an interesting *illustration* of his theological point of view? We can answer this question only by raising another: what is the source of Barth's teachings on God; whence are they derived?

It is at this point that the critics attack Barth most strongly. They declare that his theology depends on the uncritical introduction of certain arbitrary principles into Christian thought. First, there is the Reformed principle: *"Finitum non capax infiniti."* Second, there is Kierkegaard's idea of the infinite qualitative difference between time and eternity. Thirdly, there is the influence of Neo-Kantian transcendentalism which is obvious in Barth's identification of God and the "Origin." One concludes, therefore, that his teachings are dominated by metaphysical and philosophical tendencies which are essentially foreign to Christian thinking and that Barth's attack upon modern Christianity must not be taken too seriously.

There can be no doubt that there is much truth in these charges; and Barth himself has, at least partly, accepted them by refraining from using the criticized terms and concepts as frequently in his more recent writings, as in his earlier books, particularly in the *Commentary on the Romans.* He has had, however, one mighty weapon with which to defend himself; he has claimed to *depend* not on philosophical, but on Biblical authority. He has asserted that he learned his

understanding of God from the Bible. It cannot be definitely stated whether a certain philosophical and intellectual predisposition helped him to discover these
Biblical ideas which became central in his theology—
as is very possible—or whether he made use of philosophical terminology when he came to develop his
doctrines—which also is possible. But one fact is certain: he detected qualities in the Bible which had been
overlooked and neglected by modern theologians.
What he called the "Biblical attitude," the *theocentric*
orientation of the men of the Bible was doubtless
worthy of reconsideration. Thus his eyes, sharpened by
the training and upbringing of the Church of John
Calvin, beheld in a new way the sovereignty, the Lordship of God, as it is recognized particularly in the Old
Testament. God the Creator, world and man his creation—this great contrast, upon which the religion of
Israel was built, became again meaningful to Barth.
He therefore stressed the absolute superiority of God
to all creatures, the remoteness of the Creator from his
world. He reasserted with the old Israelites and the
stern Calvinists of the past the idea of the absolute obligation of man to God and of the divine judgment
which follows from the *religious* belief in a Creator.
One may say that all this is only one side of the religion of the Old Testament, that the glory of God in
nature and in man is overlooked, that Creator and
creation are unduly separated from each other.

We read, indeed, that the earth is full of God's glory
and that God created man in his own image; but we
also read about the fall in Eden and about the pains of
repentant souls who have not kept the statutes of their
Maker! The *religious* concept of a Creator—which,
by the way, does *not* necessarily imply a physical or

biological theory of the process of creation—contains a positive as well as a negative estimate of the world; and Barth emphasizes the latter. That he does so is not perhaps to the advantage of the total character of his theology and his world-view. One can, therefore, call him one-sided, but one cannot accuse him of having abused or misconstrued the creator-idea itself. It is quite possible that the world-disillusionment that befell him under the impression of the war, and his philosophical predisposition led him to this one-sidedness. At any rate, it is this belief in God which is in the background of all his thinking, and especially of his Christological idea.

Barth believes that the only possible way of thinking about God is the way taken by the men of the Bible. And upon them the meaning of God begins to shine as the boundary of mortality. "Our God is a consuming fire." "Who is there of all flesh, that hath heard the voice of the living God, and lived?" "Whether we think of Jacob or David or Jeremiah, or of Peter or Paul, there is no form nor comeliness in any aspect of them; their lives witness not to humanity but to the *end* of humanity. In the case of more than one of these men of God, one has the impression, to speak honestly, that they personally must have been quite unendurable." "Over the entrance to the Wisdom of Solomon is fixed the minatory tablet, 'Vanity of vanities, all is vanity.' The unmistakable undertone of the piety of the Psalms which people so much admire and still insist they find inspiring, is 'Lord make me to know my end, and the measure of my days, what it is; that I may know how frail I am. Behold, thou hast made my days as an handbreadth, and my age is as nothing before thee: verily every man at his best state is altogether vanity!' " [12]

On *this* background alone Jesus Christ can be fully understood. " 'The axe is laid unto the root of the trees,' *consummatio mundi*, the dissolution of all things, the passing of this age—this is the meaning of the 'Kingdom of God,' as it is preached not only by the Baptist, but by Jesus of Nazareth, by Paul and by the Apocalyptist. The work of Christ, according to the consistent synoptic, Pauline, and Johannine testimony is a type of obedience to the will of the Father that leads him straight toward death." The end of the Messiah is the question: "My God, my God, why hast thou forsaken me?" This utterance cannot be explained away. It expresses the profound sense of being lost and abandoned, *derelictio*. It means the bearing of the sins of the world. In *this* sense, the cross is the event in which in accordance with the belief in God of the Old Testament, it becomes apparent that the only source for the real, the immediate revelation of God is *death*.

Man must die in order to see God. His autonomy, his self-reliance, his certainty that he can build his life according to his dreams and speculations, his hope that he can realize his human possibilities on the basis of his understanding of himself and of his world, must be destroyed, totally destroyed, in order that he may be born to a new realism, a new objectivity, by which he can view himself and the things about him in freedom from his narrow self. Thus he is returned to his Creator. He sees things as they really are, as they are *made* to be. He is liberated from the restless desire to save himself by knowledge and by an ever growing zest to know more, which in the end must bring him to the hopeless insight that he knows *nothing*, for he knows now that he is known and with him his universe,— and that gives him rest and his growth in knowledge loses its feverishness.

Such is the wisdom of death. Such is life as seen *sub specie mortis, sub specie eterni.* And this is the *meaning* of the *theologia crucis,* which is the theology of the gospels and the Pauline letters, and of all theology nourished by them; it is the *meaning* of the belief in Jesus Christ. It is the *meaning* of the cross and the resurrection.

The cross represents the end of all *human* possibilities, but beyond it lies a possibility which does not come from man, but which must *over*come him; "Behold, I make all things new." "The affirmation of God, man, and the world given in the New Testament is based exclusively upon a possibility of a new order absolutely beyond human thought; and, therefore, as prerequisite to that order, there must come a crisis that denies all human thought." [13]

If we return now to the question as to the origin of Barth's idea of God, we can answer that he derived it from the Bible. By saying this, we have also solved the problem of Barth's Christology. He is definitely of the opinion that his view of Christ is that of the New Testament, of Paul and John as well as of the Synoptists; they saw Jesus Christ not in the light of what he was by and for himself, but on the background of his (unhistorical) relation to God. In other words Barth has returned to the faith of the early Christians. The "historical Jesus" is of as little interest to him as he was to Paul. The words and the life of this Jesus must not be interpreted in the terms of the criticisms of the lib-

eral school, but in the way of the New Testament itself. The attempts of New Testament scholars to ascertain definite facts about the historical Jesus have
ended in scepticism. On the basis of gospel-sources,
they find themselves unable to reconstruct either a
biography of Jesus or a picture of the religion that he
may have taught and personally believed. They have,
therefore, begun to look upon the gospel-records as
products of the early-Christian congregations. Only
by very difficult indirect inferences can they arrive
at the figure of Jesus himself. Barth and his friends
are in sympathy with this reorientation in the field of
New Testament research, but they recommend also
a theological reorientation in regard to Jesus. Thoroughly in accord with the methods and general viewpoint of the historical critics, they consider the books
of the New Testament as religious documents of the
Graeco-Roman world, which must be interpreted in
the light of their own Hellenistic environment. They
do not hesitate to affirm that the scholars must proceed with their work of textual criticism. The best
historical methods, they believe, will lead to the conclusion that the most significant element in earliest
Christianity was not the life of Jesus of Nazareth—as
the scholars have wanted us to believe—but the belief in his Messiahship, which revealed itself in his
death and resurrection. The apostles preached the gospel of Jesus the *Christ,* seeing him in the light of their
belief in God and concentrating their understanding
of him in the crucifixion and the resurrection. *This*
gospel of Jesus the Messiah, the Barthians are convinced, must again become the gospel of the modern
church. It is the theme of all their thinking, and their
theology is devoted to the one end of explaining the

meaning of this gospel in such a way that it can be accepted also by the man of the Twentieth Century. That is the reason why Barth speaks of God as the "Totally Other," who as the origin is the transcendental ground of all existence, as different from it as eternity is from time. All these terms are used in the hope that they, with all they imply, will recreate the setting out of which, centuries ago, the Bible developed its message.

Have we now satisfactorily answered the question whether Barth's Christology is an illustration of his own view of God or whether the latter is derived from the Christian gospel of Jesus Christ? What we have said so far is that he himself is persuaded that his idea of God is that of the Bible and that Jesus Christ is the fulfilment of this Biblical view. However, with this answer, illuminating as it may be, we have not exhausted the question. It could have been differently phrased, and then its real point would have been more definitely brought out: Is the historical event which is signified by the name Jesus Christ the basis of Barth's theology and does its truth depend upon this historical fact—or would it be true also without Jesus? Did God reveal himself in Jesus Christ in Palestine, sometime about the year 30, or has he revealed and does he reveal himself *whenever* the crisis of life becomes apparent? Did God reveal himself once and for all in the death of Jesus or does he reveal himself in the death of all human aspirations and possibilities? Barth himself answers,[14] "Jesus is God's existentiality in the light of his contingency. All Rationalism is destroyed by the *skandalon* of the historical revelation of the Christ. God is not a 'rational truth.' His eternity is not the harmless, unparadoxical, direct, universal validity of

general ideas (the God-*idea*, the Christ-*idea*, the me-
diator-*idea, etc.*) . . . God is personality, once, contingent, unique (*Der Einmalige, der Einige, der Ein-
zigartige*) and as such the eternal and omnipotent
one, nothing else. The proof of this is Jesus, the human, historical Jesus. But Jesus is the *Christ.* As such
he is God's contingency in the light of his existentiality. Therefore, we contrast to all believing and unbelieving Historism and Psychologism the *skandalon* of
an eternal revelation in Jesus, a revelation of that
which Abraham and Plato certainly had already seen.
God is no 'accidental historical truth.' With an abrupt
Never! and Ever! the act of his hand is removed from
mythologizing and pragmatization, from story-tell-
ing. It is exactly in Jesus that God's love cuts through
all historical psychological indirectnesses and media-
cies; it is not bound to this and that, there and here.
The Eternal and Almighty One is also the contingent
and unique one. The proof of this is Jesus the Christ,
the eternal Christ. God's own son stands where the
roads cross each other, and nowhere else." Jesus Christ,
as the revealer of God is neither a historical fact nor a
universal truth, and he is a historical fact *and* a universal truth. And the God whom he reveals made
himself known in Palestinian events about the year
30, but he revealed himself as the eternal one to all
who could read the signs of their times before these
events took place. The truths of Rationalism and of
Historism are here both affirmed and denied. God is a
God of historical singularity as well as of eternal universality. In Jesus Christ eternity became time (God
became man), and in Jesus Christ eternity cut into
the world of time, causing its radical crisis (this man
died the death of the cross). Here we have belief in

the Jesus of history *and* in the Christ of faith. Only in Jesus, and in the crucified Jesus, is God to be found, and yet God is never confined to a single historical fact. He is both *Deus revelatus* and *Deus absconditus,* both revealed and hidden. God is in Jesus Christ as an *unhistorical event.* He belongs to the world as the tangent belongs to the circle, never *and* ever.

We could continue citing such paradoxical statements. What do they mean? One can speak of God's revelation only in dialectical terms. "Jesus Christ"— even these two words are dialectic. Jesus as a historical fact is insignificant and not absolute. The idea of Christ is unimportant and not absolutely true. But "Jesus Christ" means that the absolute God has become a historical fact and that the single event of history is charged with absolute truth; in him God's eternity is contingent.

The problem of history and faith which has been in the center of modern theological discussion is here seen in a new light. It cannot be solved either by making faith dependent upon a single historical fact or by eliminating the significance of history from the realm of faith. But history and faith must be seen in their dialectical relationship. The Christian affirms that God lives in a light no man can approach unto, and he believes that this God has revealed himself. No historical and no rational thinking can explain this conviction; the only adequate way of speaking about God is the dialectical one. God, if he is God, is everywhere, never limited to a contingent historical incident; but this eternal God disclosed himself—according to the belief of the Christian who accepts the testimony of the founders of his church—in Jesus Christ. In his light we see the light—that is all that can be said; and the only way to say it is in dialectical, paradoxical terms. All great Christian theologians—notably Luther and Calvin—had, for this reason, to speak of Jesus Christ.

It must be plain that the most significant factor in this understanding of Christianity is *faith*. One who has no faith must hear all this with deaf ears. For there is no way of compelling a man to accept this gospel of God, unless the holy spirit has influenced his heart and given him faith.

Well, then—does the truth of the Christian message depend upon faith, an attitude or function which is purely human after all? What is faith? It is first of all obedience, which is a sense for the specifically divine, for the "Totally Other" in God. Under fear and trembling it originates from the perception that God is God. "Faith means to 'fear and love God as he is and not as we conceive him. It involves submission under the judgment, the crisis, which characterizes the general situation between God and man. This crisis consists in the fact that we cannot grasp or conceive God, and that he is and remains for us the absolutely other, strange, unknown, unapproachable.' [15] Faith is, therefore, never a belief on the basis of which it might be said what God is. Neither is it ever identical with inner experience, the qualities of which would disclose the essence of the divine. If faith is faith *in God*, it must be *vacuum, Hohlraum.*" [16] This characterization of faith as a vacuum has often been misunderstood. How can we even speak of God, one asks, if not on the basis of experience? If one interprets experience as a "*Widerfahrnis,*" as an acknowledgment of something that happens to man, as a reaction to something that must be recognized. accepted, *passively* received, Barth would not object to the term and its application to faith. But if experience is identified with an inner sensation, or feeling, or with a belief and its psychological content, he rises in rebellion; and calls faith, by contrast, a vacuum. Faith in God, he proclaims, cannot be a psychological fact. Nor are any psychological conditions of an intellectual or aesthetic nature to be fulfilled before we can attain faith. From the human point of view, it is always a "jump into emptiness." [17] It is devotion to something that is not seen, that is ever unknown. If faith in God grows into a *belief about God*, if devotion to the totally other God is narrowed to devotion to a definitely circumscribed purpose or ideal, it has ceased to be faith. For God and man are then no longer seen in their transcendental relation. God has then become a human, psychological element. In order to guard himself against such a misinterpretation, Barth describes faith as a vacuum. It can be filled only by the eternal God himself.

Only after man has relinquished all certainty of religious achievement, only after he has torn all masks of piety or piously living from his face, can he grasp the objectivity of God.[18] Only when he finds himself in a situation of brokenness, only when he is on the verge of bankruptcy, only when he discovers himself on the edge of the pit of despair, is he ready to venture the jump into the realm of uncertainty. Then and then only is he capable of believing that he is held by the hand of the eternal God—that God is loyal. He is then ready to believe in the Lord Jesus Christ and in his resurrection, thus sharing the faith of the Apostles who, when they proclaimed the Lordship of Jesus, were pointing to his crucifixion, to his end ("My God, my God, why hast Thou forsaken me!"), and not to any religious achievement of his prophetic career. Their belief that Christ had risen was their interpretation of the significance of his death in the light of the eternal God of whom the prophets of the Old Testament had spoken. This interpretation, however, Barth would say, must not be attributed to their religious ingenuity, as if they were thus attempting to save themselves and the pious notions they had inherited, but rather to their recognition of the sovereignty of God, which asserts itself in the judgment over all being, "revealing a deep, secret 'Yes' in the 'No' " (Luther). Man and his world must, therefore, partake of the death of Jesus Christ, in order to rise with him. To die in the Lord is to live in the Lord. If we want to have God, we are bidden as men to die. In no other way can sinners be justified.

In this case, of course, justification cannot be a fact with which one can reckon or upon which one may rely as upon a definite certainty. It is not a growth or an ethical development. It occurs always anew, whenever human possibilities have been emptied, whenever man has reached the point of complete despair as to the beliefs and values upon which he has built his life. He is compelled to distinguish himself from himself, to give up the ideals which he has held in order to become a new man—a new man not by embracing new ideals in place of the old ones, since they too would have to be surrendered, but by acknowledging that by facing nothingness he has become free from himself and is enabled to begin life on an entirely new level. But as long as he exists in this world as a man, he can never hope to *enjoy* this new state. The newness, the salvation, will always be before him. Again and again he will have to break down, in order to rise and march

on. His despair is thus a *desperatio fiducialis,* and the
faith upon which he lives is definitely eschatological.
His unity with God is unattainable as long as he is
limited to his human existence. The world of God
touches his world only at a mathematical point, as a
tangent a circle—the point where, when free from
himself, he recognizes that nothing but the sovereignty
of the supremely "Other" can liberate him from himself. This *desperatio fiducialis,* this *futurum resurrectionis* is the only content or result of faith, as the disciples of Jesus Christ themselves discovered, in considering his fate. Since that time we have seen the light in
his light.

Here again it is evident that for Barth theological
thinking is ethical, existential thinking. It is well to
remember that he expounded all these thoughts not
because he desired to add another commentary to the
numerous others already in use or because he wanted
to add his theological wisdom to that of other scholars,
but because he had to speak of a practical need. Of this
need he had become oppressingly aware when Sunday
after Sunday he preached to people who, as he was
forced to believe, did not come to hear *his* opinions
on life and its various problems or to receive guidance
from *him* in moral or intellectual troubles, but to be
told about the fundamental conflict of their existence,
a conflict they were conscious of whenever their own
individual worlds clashed with those of others, whenever they were shaken out of their dreams of self-
sufficiency, whenever they were awakened from their
complacent solitariness, from their "being by themselves."

The impact of the Christian gospel as he understood
it in the light of this situation, was not a healing of

this distress of living, but the radical confirmation of
it; not a return into a new dream of righteousness,
self-righteousness, glorified and embellished by the
uplifting, refining, sweetening, inspiring emotions of
religion, but the turning away from any sort of dependence upon belief for the sake of concentration
upon God, whose eternal "Otherness" had been revealed in the crisis of existence. Repentance—radical,
thorough change of mind—he discovered, was the
meaning of the gospel.

*This word "repentance" contains Barth's entire
theology and ethics.* For that reason his thinking is
truly Christian, early-Christian. It is eschatological. It
is hope, not possession. It involves an unworldliness, an
anti-worldliness, a criticism of everything that comes
to rest in itself, of everyone who has the courage to
claim a *having*. It leads to an attack particularly upon
the church, because the church so seldom produces
"repentance in fear and trembling, reverence before
God." When has the church maintained its distance
from the eternal, when assailed (religious) man, or
loosened the structure of human existence? When has
it educated to absolute objectivity, to an incorrupti-
ble endurance and perseverance in the perplexity
which God gives us? It plans instead to give a kind
of certainty and security, which in critical times (witness the War!) often prove unreliable and anything
but the absolutes they are supposed to be.

When, in concluding this analysis of the thoughts
of the *Commentary on the Romans,* we devote our
attention finally to the ethical problem, we are concerned with Barth's chief interest. He has expressed
himself most clearly on this point:[19] "The problem of
ethics is the explicit reminder and injunction that the

subject of the discussion about God is not something objective—or supernatural (*Über-oder Hinterwelt*) —not a metaphysics, nor a treasure of inner experiences, nor a transcendent "unfathomable deep," but the life of man as we know it in nature and culture, especially in so far as the one who is engaged in the discussion has to live in a necessarily concrete fashion. The emergence of the ethical problem is the safeguard of the frequently emphasized existentiality of the concepts used in this discussion, the guarantee that the formula 'God himself, God alone' which we have repeated to the point of fatigue does not designate a divine 'something' or an ideality opposite us, but the inscrutable divine *relation* in which we, as men, find ourselves. These concepts and formulae in their unhuman and unworldly abstractness originate in the life of man in a world full of commotion and tension, and their abstraction could not be worse misunderstood than by being conceived as 'absolute' (dissolved) from their object and not constantly relative (referring) to the concreteness of our every-day life. The reading of all distinctly worldly literature, especially the newspapers, is urgently recommended for understanding the *Epistle to the Romans. For thinking, if it is genuine, is thinking of life and therefore and therein thinking of God.*"

The ethical attitude which results from the recognition of God is, therefore, one which relates all doings in the world of time to the eternal, to the total "Otherness" of God. It does not result in a programme for a new sort of activity in the reconstruction of life, but in the acknowledgment that God causes a radical disturbance of man's life, particularly in its heights, achievements and successes. "Christianity does not like

to hear too loud and too confident words about the
evolution of the world; the completed or planned de-
velopments and constructions of science, technique,
art, morality and religion; physical and mental health;
prosperity and welfare; the splendors and gratifying
features of marriage, family, church, state, society.
. . . It is rarely a party to the erection of monuments.
It suspects therein always . . . idolatry." Neither cultural optimism nor asceticism, but the recognition of
all things in their relativeness, this is the tendency of
the Christian mind. Viewing the world *sub specie
mortis* makes it appear as an index finger, pointing to
the eternal. All that activity is ethical, therefore, that
somehow does not fit into the "scheme of this world"
(Rom. XI, 2.), but within it bears witness to the
strangeness of God. If the term "love of God" describes the attitude of one who lives in the holy spirit,
then such love is definable as the profoundest objectivity possible toward the *Problems* of our life. "When
man is . . . unescapably struck by the question: who
am I? he loves God. For the opposite "thou" which
forces man to distinguish himself from himself, is
God, and compelled thus to distinguish himself from
himself, man has already practiced his love of God." [20]
We may perhaps best interpret the ethical attitude
which Barth here recommends by calling it "disinter-
estedness," a negation of selfish concerns without the
destruction of that something which constitutes a
self. Barth often paraphrases the process by the use
of the grammatical terms subject and predicate. The
predicate is changed, but the subject remains the
same.

There is no hope for a construction of a system of
ethical virtues in the name of Christianity. The Chris-

tian religion calls only for an openmindedness toward
the true nature of life in this world. Its crisis must be
bravely and honestly faced and borne. Only then is
God given the glory. This is not the ethical, or rather
unethical, principle of resignation, but the most truly
ethical motive of constant and continuous renewal.
It is made concrete to each one of us in our relationship with our neighbors. In the fact that man faces
man we have the puzzle of the "original state of nature." By the singleness of the "other man," one is
reminded of his own singleness, or rather of his solitariness, which by being absolutized grows into self-sufficiency, so that life often is nothing but a monologue.
The discovery of the neighbor, however, may also
lead to the discovery of God, if namely "we see and
hear in every temporal 'thou' which we are told to
love, the opposite eternal 'thou' without which there
is no 'I'." After we have once come to the realization
that God must be God and that he must be God for
us, we are liberated from the blindness of individualism or subjectivism in any form, for we are then willing to throw ourselves upon him, the "Totally Other."
Our neighbor helps us to make concrete this new orientation: he as "the other" is the simile, the parable of
the "One"—God. In loving him, therefore, we love
God; and the love of God—the art of distinguishing
ourselves from ourselves—is practiced in our attitude
toward our neighbor.

Whether we have done justice to Barth's *Römerbrief* we cannot say. Naturally, it is impossible in a
brief chapter to have given expression to all that the
weighty volume compasses. Much of the theological
discussion has been neglected. We have not concerned

ourselves, for instance, with its interpretations of the doctrines of original sin and predestination. Our main purpose has been to catch its general tenor and fundamental point of view.

We are well aware, however, that we may be liable to encounter criticism not because of the omission of certain significant ideas but because of general misinterpretation. It is quite possible that some one, well acquainted with Barth and the Barthians, will rise to say: Have you not forgotten that Barth is a dialectical theologian? Have you not made him a mystic, whose approach to God is the *via negativa,* by which he negates all that is human for the purpose of ascending to God, the ineffable, unknown One? Have you not made Barth speak of man in such a way that his own criticism of the mystic, which you yourself mentioned in the preceding chapter, would apply also to him? Have you not presented Barth as if he wanted us to be "men with a vengeance," in spite of the fact that he himself declares that there is no salvation in that?

We realize that these questions are fair. We admit that in our discussion we have given no room to the words "redemption," "forgiveness," "grace," "justification," "certainty of salvation" and to their meaning and significance in Christian thought and life. They express the benefits which a Christian derives from the fact that God has really and truly revealed himself, that "God has become man." We cannot deny that they frequently occur in the "Römerbrief." Are we then wrong in our analysis of it? Have we then willfully neglected to stress all those phases of Christian belief which on the basis of the divine act of revelation give expectation of sanctification, renewal of life—and

that in spite of the fact that Barth has not failed to
do them justice? Have we unduly emphasized the
"crisis" in the "theology of crisis?" Have we heard
only its call to "repentance" and not its good tidings
of the "Kingdom of God?" Have we misrepresented
Barth as if in his understanding, God the Father and
the Lord Jesus Christ and the Holy Spirit did not grant
healing of the pains of man and salvation from his
sin and sinfulness? Is not man, according to *our* discussion of the "Römerbrief," constantly kept advised
of his lack of redemption, of his brokenness just *because* he is aware of the divine?

We do not believe that we have been mistaken in
stressing *this* as the outstanding feature of Barth's
book. *This* crisis, *this* thorough, radical *disillusionment* of man and his religious, philosophical, cultural,
and social beliefs in so far as they are based on his religious, rational and social *autonomy—is* the meaning,
the tendency of Barth's *Commentary.* Are we then
to suppose that agnosticism, that scepticism is the
goal at which we finally arrive if we follow our guide
to the end of his road? Is he a prophet of destruction,
of some sort of Nihilism? Yes, a prophet, that is what
he is, even a prophet of destruction, but—a *true*
prophet, nevertheless. He speaks of the fall of the Babel
Tower of modern "religion," because he *knows* of
someone that cannot, that will never fall. He does not
lead us to the "nothing," but to the "origin." He does
not prophecy the end of religion because he is obsessed
by the lust to unveil as illusion what secretly has long
been held as such, or because he enjoys the grim spec-
tacle of parading the shaky relativistic "standpoints"
of modern man as meaningless and empty puppets before the eyes of his baffled contemporaries. He is not

a victim of war-psychology, who after having experienced the cataclysm of his ideals, now proceeds, in a rage of despair and discouragement, to throw the sum total of life into the pit of broken hopes and joys. On the contrary, because he has been awed by eternity, because he has heard its thunders and seen its lightnings, he has become "a voice in the wilderness," speaking of judgment over time, calling to repentance. He shouts his "No" to the "realities" of this world, because he knows of the "Yes" which is not of this world. Frantically he points to this firm pole. Nothing must be in the way of those who want to see it. He therefore knocks down everything that obstructs the view. The King of Glory shall come in. There cannot, shall not be any other glory but his.

Is it only another illusion? The fever, high fever of a mortal illness? Is that it? No, says Barth, it is a new attention to that of which alone the Bible is witness. It is the recovery of the "Biblical attitude." It is the re-discovery of the cause for the sake of which those strange, awkward figures of history, the prophets of Israel and the apostles of Christ lived their unhuman, unworldly lives. The Barthian theology of the *Römerbrief* bears new testimony to that "revelation" which is the concern of the men of the Bible. We hope that our discussion has not failed to make that impression.

How is such a thing possible? Have not the last fifty or even hundred years seen the rise of a "new theology?" And has this new theology not shown us the "*historical Jesus*" and "*historical Christianity*," giving to history what belongs to history, definitely relegating to the past what is of the past? It has undeniably done so—and now we shall listen again to a contemporary who claims authority in the name of that "past."

But such a description does not treat Barth fairly. It is he who returns the historical Jesus to history. He does not speak in *his* name. And yet—his positive message points back to Christ, Jesus Christ. How can this be? Is he both a disciple and a traitor to Jesus, both John *and* Judas Iscariot? Is he a worshiper of Christ *and* Antichrist? Is he a "Christian" unbeliever, a sceptic who still hangs on to what inwardly he has lost?

Again we begin to ask doubting questions. The *Römerbrief* does not answer them. In another, more recent book, *The Dogmatics,* our problem is frankly faced. We must, therefore, now devote our attention to *its* theses.

VI

BARTHIANISM AS A NEW THEOLOGY: PRINCIPLES

THE first volume of Barth's "Dogmatics" bears the title *The Doctrine of the Word of God, Prolegomena to Christian Dogmatics.* It is an introduction to a system of Christian theology, and discusses the requirements that must be fulfilled before one can approach the task of outlining a theology. Other Protestant theologians who are authors of works on Christian dogmatics have also devoted themselves to "Prolegomena," before they proceeded to unfold their "systems." But their approach differs radically from Barth's. He does not follow the example of his fellow theologians in presenting a general philosophy of religion before he outlines the Christian doctrines, but establishes the "doctrine of the Word of God," thereby anticipating in the "Prologue" much of what is to be dealt with in the main section. He does not investigate the meaning of religion in general or the possibility of the belief in God, in order to devote himself to the Christian religion. He makes a much more concrete and simple assumption. He proposes to think systematically on the basis of the fact that Christian preaching is going on. "There is Christian dogmatics, because there is Christian speech." [1] Dogmatics is then "the striving for the understanding of the legitimate content of Christian speech concerning God and man."

His question is what makes Christian preaching Christian. This seems a unique conception of theology, but it is doubtless justified by the history and the practice of the church. Barth rightly calls attention to the fact from which all Christian dogma has issued, the simple fact that there is preaching, that men have preached and preached differently, so that the question as to the truth or error, purity or impurity, edification or lack of edification of what pretended to be the Christian message simply had to emerge. The preaching of the Christian cause and the human fallibility involved in this preaching was the occasion for the development of dogmas.

What, then, is "Christian preaching"? Barth calls attention to three characteristic features of the true sermon:[2]

The first characteristic is speech in accordance with a *commission*. "A Christian does not speak . . . of God and of man, because he wants to do so; nor does he choose what he wants to say; he speaks because he is under a compulsion . . . in regard to the 'that' as in regard to the 'what.' "

The second characteristic is speech which must be accounted for—*i.e., universally valid*. "A Christian does not speak of God and man unauthoritatively, with the presumption of expressing only an opinion (*opinio*, δόχα) : he speaks with the presumption of speaking the truth according to his best knowledge and conscience."

The third characteristic is *credible* speech. "Credible means worthy of belief." "A Christian does not speak of God and man in the way of a smart *conversateur* who demands only to be listened to, or of a teacher who expects merely attention and understanding, or of an agitator who desires nothing but applause, or of a person who is satisfied as long as he is listened to submissively and respectfully. He considers his speech worthy to be believed."

Christian speech is not the utterance of an opinion, not a lecture, not a disputation, not advice, but the proclamation, κήευγμα, of something that as truth is valid for all; it makes the unique claim, by the means of human words, of promulgating God's word. The content of Christian preaching is God's speech, God's word. As related to God, the sermon does not deal with something divine which may exist by itself, but refers to the one God who is so concretely present that he must be spoken of. It is not as if the words of the preacher could control the fact of God in any way, for these words are entirely at the disposal of God, who can never be controlled or mastered. Many a sermon, to be sure, does not directly reveal this sovereignty of God, but somehow the divine authority asserts itself whenever human words point to the unspeakable "Otherness" and supremacy which is hinted at in the word "God." *All* preaching of God is, therefore, a daring endeavor, which would be less lightheartedly undertaken, if the awareness of its fundamental difference from every other sort of speech were present in the mind of the preacher. Preaching demands submission to an imperative. It can be done only if there is a commission, a compulsion to do so. *Christian* preaching is undertaken because it recognizes the imperative in the testimony of the prophets and the apostles. "There would be no such thing as

Christian preaching if the testimony of the apostles and prophets were not given. It responds to that testimony. Its essence is to accept it, to make it live again in the present." [3]

The words of the prophets and apostles of the Bible are the authority for the sermon of the Christian church. But why? Because these words bear witness to the revelation of God. The historical tradition of the message of the men of the Bible is authoritative for the Christian church only because it points to the superhistorical revelation of God. It is no *"Paulus dixit"* ("Paul said") that is the imperative which the Christian church obeys, but the *"Deus dixit" in* the words of Paul. The Word in the words of the Bible, God's word behind the words of the apostles, the revelation without which the testimony of the apostles could not have been given—this is the authority of Christian preaching. The sermon, therefore, is a "proclamation of God's word, and as such is possible only when the revelation is received of which the Scripture is a witness or when the Scripture is received which gives testimony of the revelation." [4]

These three factors in the appearance of the Word of God—the original, superhistorical (*urgeschichtliche*) *revelation*, the *Scripture*, and the *sermon*—must be kept in mind if the dogmatic question what is legitimate Christian preaching, is to be answered. Upon them Barth builds his system of dogmatic Prolegomena and the three main chapters of his book deal severally with them. It is easy to understand why the problem of revelation is paramount in his discussion, for it is the basis on which the sermon as well as theology stands. This first volume on dogmatics is, therefore, really a treatise on the idea of revelation. It

is very significant for us to note this fact, for our analysis of Barthian thinking has as yet not proffered a
clear and satisfactory conception of what kind of revelation it is that underlies the theology of crisis. We
should also observe that in this first large book after
the *Römerbrief*, Barth has not deviated from the primary issues which led him originally into the fight for
a new Christian theology. His chief concern is still
the sermon, and the Bible is still the norm of preaching. The peculiar understanding of God and of man in
relation with God, which he unfolded in the stormy
passages of the *Römerbrief*, is still in evidence. It is
brought into play immediately after the definition of
"dogmatics" is given.

The ideas on the sermon so far presented are the result of what Barth calls the "phenomenological," *i.e.*
descriptive method. After this has served its purpose
to explain what Christian preaching is and ought to
be, it is dismissed and replaced by another way of
thinking, which is called *existential*. By this he calls
attention to the fact that one cannot treat of preaching without thinking of the man who does it, nor of
the sermon without referring to the person who hears
it. In other words, the dogmatician cannot deal with
the word of God without relating it to the man to
whom it is addressed. He ceases to be an objective ob-
server or spectator; his own whole existence becomes
involved in the thought. He must ask himself two
questions. First, how is it possible, how does one dare,
to preach the word of God?; second, how can one
hear it?

If one is willing to take the risk of preaching about
God, he encounters his first chief difficulty when he
is asked how he *knows* about God, of whom he is to

speak. Barth dismisses as unsatisfactory the usual answers of modern theologians. He claims that their
argument on the basis of the religious *experience* is
untenable. "What is knowledge of God," he asks, "if,
in order to be certain of it, I have . . . . to attribute
an *a priori* content to my religious experience, if I
have . . . to consider myself one who possesses the specific content of Christian experience, or one who
has experienced something 'incomparable' or 'irrefutable,' or discovered in *himself* an 'unchangeableness'
or 'absolute ground' of existence—at the bottom of
his personality the absolute personality of God—or
perceived himself as 'absolutely dependent' or 'absolutely free' or . . . if I even claim to partake of God's
self-consciousness. How can one say such things! How
can I possibly conclude that I have knowledge of the
divine, if such presuppositions have to be made, if I
have to say things of myself which, plainly, are sim--
ply not true?" [5] If these analyses are really correct,
one can only arrive at one of two conclusions: Either
he discovers he does not reach *God* on the basis of such
experiences, but only an object among other objects,
a part of the world; or he gives up the thought that a
human being capable of experiencing God, exists, for
there is no man, woman, or child that could claim to
have the spirit of God.

It is plain that Barth is arguing here on the basis of
a concept of God which accords with that of his former works. The infinite qualitative difference between
time and eternity, between God and man is here too
presupposed. The definitions of the modern theologians are measured by this concept. It must be re-
marked, however, that, although Barth is generally
right in characterizing the modern approach to God

as subjectivism, he has failed to notice that many of the scholars whom he criticizes correlate the experiencing human subject and the experienced divine object in such a way that the possibility of knowing does not entirely depend upon the experience of the knowing person, but *also* on the objectivity, or shall we say accessibility, of God, who is to be known. In another connection we shall return to this problem.

Let us now suppose that there were a way of knowing of God. How could one then have the courage to speak of him? "Whosoever dares to speak of God, must take his chances with God alone, for there is a definite, very actual estrangement between God and everything in the world that is great and interesting, whereof one might possibly dare speak without much courage. The case would be different, if one could put one of the gods in the place of God, if one were to set up, as God, all-ruling Eros, or the miracle of the occult life, or the German (or American) God, or the spirit of progress. But if there were one who really knew God, him who is God above all other gods, not to be compared and not to be exchanged with any other, who cannot enter into competition or covenant with the greatest or smallest in nature, history, culture, or civilization that might pretend to be divine —how thoroughly would *he* be silenced! Into what impossible solitariness, remote from the highway of the many, as well as from the quiet paths of the noblest and finest, would *he* have to go who really knew God and dared to speak of him!" [6] And if one dare speak of him, from whom has he received the right?

Impossible—that is the answer to the question, How *can* I preach? And yet, preaching takes place. Must it then be supposed that the preachers are unaware of the impossibility of their task? Many, many undoubtedly are. And the others? They do the impossible because they must; because they are commissioned, ordered to speak of God.

Barth does not reveal what this commission is and how it is brought to the preacher, but he claims that since the authority to preach cannot be found in human experience, it must be divine. He thus jumps rather abruptly to a new definition of the "Word of God." It is this: God is and remains *subject* in his Word. *Deus dixit.* He speaks of himself. And "the Christian preacher speaks because of the fact that God speaks of himself." [7]

We are led to another and yet similar conclusion if we ask, How can we hear of God? It is in answer to this question that Barth returns in the *Dogmatics* to the fundamental thought of the *Römerbrief.* "Human existence is a question. It is a continuous stream of conflicts and contradictions. Again and again man would like to settle down, but again and again he must march on—without a homestead either among the angels or among the animals, either in the soul or in the body, either in the spirit or in nature, either in the infinite or in the finite, either in thought or in the world of the senses, either in the 'I' or in the 'Not-I'... Why so? Precisely because he is by himself. He is always both with, and remote from, God, and that not peacefully, not in synthesis, but always with one relationship under the crushing contradiction of the other, always so that he cannot enjoy the one because of the other." [8] In such and similar moving words is described the situation of contrasts in human existence. And then this amazing conclusion is reached: "This contrast is humanity. It is the exile to which he who hears

of God and his relation with man, finds himself con-
signed. Perhaps, in pious contempt of the world or in
worldly contempt of piety, he has tried all or almost
all that can be tried with the body against the soul,
with the spirit against nature, with the finite as opposed to the infinite, with life as if there were no death
—or vice versa. Perhaps he has not yet experienced the
vanity of all these attempts. However that may be, he
is torn within himself, he moves in a circle—whether
he begins from right or left, from below or above. He,
his existence, has become a question to him, since he has
heard of God, really of God: of *God*—*i.e.*, of the Lord
above the conflicts of his existence, of the one who
really exists, because he is in the synthesis. He has heard
of God, with whom he *should* be at home in order to
be himself, and with whom he is not at home, so that,
lacking in synthesis, his existence becomes one single
question." [9]

The conclusion which we have called amazing is
the idea that this questionable, unredeemed character of human existence is discovered *because* one has
heard of God. We should expect that the consciousness of the conflicts of human life would be prior
to the consciousness of hearing of God, that the question as to the unity of life would result from the search
for the answer, that the finding of the answer in God
would follow the question. But Barth declares that the
answer is prior to the question, that the question
emerges in man only because he has heard the answer.
How shall we understand this? Are we to assume that
Barth presents here the solution given by idealistic,
speculative philosophy? He strenuously objects to such
an assumption, by pointing out that, if that were true,
the question would be but seemingly asked; for a ques-

tion the answer of which is already known cannot be a
real one. The person who claims to know the unity of
his life deceives himself, for in reality he lives always
in conflict within himself. No synthesis, no solution,
which he could bestow upon himself because of *his a
priori* knowledge of it would be true, for it is he, thoroughly he himself, who lives in the tension, and he
cannot extricate *himself* from it. Salvation must come
from without, from one who is wholly other than he.
And only when he hears *him,* does he become really,
concretely aware of the dilemma of his existence. But
the "other" must always remain the "other." As soon
as he ceased to be that, he would be drawn into the
human conflict. To hear of God, therefore, can never
be identical with salvation or security. The preaching
of God can never extinguish the restlessness of the
"question of existence." It rather confirms it. Hearing the Word of God does not answer the quest for
unity, for the meaning of life, but evokes it. The answer is God's and not man's. Hearing the Word of God
is to hear God speak, is to come under the spell of God's
revelation. But *this* revelation is of the hidden, foreign,
remote God; God *remains* to man the wholly other.
Man may know of his salvation, but as long as he is
man he cannot possess it. Answer and question can
never become one.

But man would not ask the question if he had not
heard the answer. He would not seek God if he had not
found him. He would not know of the conflict between spirit and flesh, if he did not know of God's
peace. He would not be aware of his need, if he had not
heard of God's mercy. God's is the initiative.

These thoughts may be reviewed under a twofold
aspect: In the first place, can they not be related to

idealistic dialectic? If I did not know of the synthesis,
a conflict between thesis and antithesis would not occur to me. If I did not have an *a priori* knowledge of
God, I would not seek him. And in the second, do they
not remind us of the gospel which exhorts us to love
God because he has first loved us?

It seems as if Barth makes use of both idealistic philosophy and the gospel, but in a very peculiar way,
which is best described by his own preference for the
Calvinist dictum: *Finitum non capax infiniti*, or by his
fondness for Kierkegaard's sentence regarding the infinite qualitative difference between time and eternity,
which was the theme of the *Römerbrief*. Fundamentally oriented to the thought implied in these words, he
regards the "synthesis" not as immanent, but as absolutely transcendent and the love of God likewise. In
other words: his discussion retains the mood of idealistic ethics as well as of the gospel, but at the same time
shatters it. We think we know what Barth is saying
when he uses Pascal's word "Thou wouldst not seek
God, hadst thou not already found him;" but when he
reminds us that God is never object, but always subject, that *we* do not find him, but that *he* finds us,
that we would not ask the question, had he not first
given the answer, we are baffled.

Our bewilderment is cleared up, when we are informed that we could not hear God, had he not first
spoken to us. We can understand that. We are glad to
be told that Jesus Christ is this Word of God, that he
is his revelation. We are still more relieved when we
are definitely advised to remember that this revelation
took place in the years 1–30 A.D., in Palestine. But
we are again thrown into disturbance by the verdict
that all this is the revelation of a God who is hidden,

a revelation not of history, but of super-history, not to be known as other historical facts are to be known, but only by and in itself.

As soon as we imagine we have grasped the meaning, it has escaped from us. Our only consolation is our recollection of the thought that God is God and not man: the "Wholly Other" must always be unknown to us. We can hear him, but we cannot make him our own. So we remain just what we are. God, or the Word of God, is never a reality for us.

But why should we then concern ourselves about him? If God is Lord over the conflicts of life, if he is peace, harmony, synthesis, we cannot but be eager to have him *our* God. It is true that we are Christians because we believe that in Jesus Christ the God of peace has become "God with us," Immanuel. Barth too considers himself a Christian. He too believes that in Jesus Christ the Almighty has become God for us. It is the theme of theology to unfold this gospel. He too desires to be engaged in unfolding such a theology.

But how can he do so?

We must review the arguments of Barth which we have already discussed. By the phenomenological method, he has arrived at the conclusion that Christian preaching takes place on the authority of the revelation of God to which the Scripture bears witness. The single word of God occurring alike in revelation, Scripture, and preaching, is, therefore, the theme of dogmatic theology. This principle established, he switches to another method of discussion which he calls the existential, intending thereby to include man in the theological totality as he really is. Temporarily he forgets his former definition of the Word of God, by which he has explained that if God is to be preached, man cannot do it, but only God himself. The same argument applied to the problem whether God can be heard should lead to the conclusion that man cannot hear him. Barth, to be sure, reaches this conclusion, but he adds to it another thought. He declares that as man becomes aware of the unredeemed, conflict-burdened nature of his existence, he does hear God. We can explain this contradiction only if we suppose that Barth uses two concepts of God: One that God is absolute transcendence; and the second that God is what we seek when the conflicting realities of life are incomprehensible to us as to their meaning. These two concepts of God Barth usually combines in one. His emphasis on the first prevents him from joining the camp of Idealists into which consistent adherence to the second one would lead him. For if he were to follow its logic he would finally be compelled to admit that knowledge of God is identical with an *a priori* knowledge of the *meaning* of life, represented, for instance, by the ideas of beauty, truth and goodness, by loyalty to which man could trust himself to overcome the conflict of his life. But Barth does *not* follow this logic. Again and again he drills into our minds that our life is and remains a question—*i.e.*, lacking meaning, and that the answer—*i.e.*, attainment of meaning, belongs to a plane radically different from ours. The answer is present with us only in so far as it causes the crisis. That is the meaning of Barth's constantly reiterated assertion that God's revelation is disclosure of his concealment or hiddenness.

This, then, is the structure of what Barth calls existential thinking about the word of God. But it is only one focus of his theology. The other is the emphasis on the *revelation of God in Jesus Christ*. Again we arrive

at the problem of the relation of these two chief
themes. We have struggled with it before. The more
thoroughly we discuss the issues of the Barthian
theology, the clearer must be the conviction, that it is
not such thinking as could be compared with the
movement of a circle around its one central point; it
is rather analogous to the movement of an ellipse
around its two foci. We will do well to remember that
these two foci have already appeared in Barth's own
first description of the beginnings of his theological
revolution, when, in speaking of the preacher's difficulties, he referred, on the one hand, to his concern
for the lives of his hearers in their infinite contradiction, and, on the other, to his task of preaching the
Biblical word. We also recollect that we finished the
discussion of the *Römerbrief* with the question as to
how Barth's philosophy of life might be reconciled
with his claim to present true Christian theology.

Let us not think that with these explanations and
recollections we have solved anything. We have but
restated the problem. For if any one should be under
the impression that Christian theological thinking is
centered in but one theme, he is mistaken. Christian
theology has always had two foci. Its task has been to
keep them both in place. The relation between God
there *and* man here has been its theme. We must be
grateful to Barth for bringing this out so definitely.
The question is whether his is the only possible Christian "theological ellipse." What authority has he for
the claim that the transcendent God whose revelation
discloses to us that *we* as men cannot know him, and,
therefore, that we lack redemption, is the Father of
Jesus Christ, of whom the Bible speaks? Our further

analysis of the *Dogmatics* ought to enable us to find an answer.

Before we proceed let us review the problem from still another angle. The fundamental problem of the Christian theologian is the revelation of God in Jesus Christ; for the gospel upon which the church is founded is the invitation to all men to believe in this revelation and to live accordingly. In the second chapter of this book we dealt with the history of theology in view of this problem. We discovered that the concepts of revelation offered by the theologians of the past were unsatisfactory. When some interpreted the fact of revelation as the appearance of the supernatural God in Jesus Christ or as the supernatural inspiration of the Bible, they based their argument on a principle which is out of accord with the understanding of the laws of nature as we now possess it. When others explained the fact of revelation on the basis of the modern philosophies of nature and man, they did not do justice to the Christian belief that God has revealed himself in Jesus Christ and in no one else. The supernaturalistic concept of revelation cannot convincingly show that God became *man,* the naturalistic (psychological or historical) concept of revelation fails to explain that God—really God—became man. The first view represents Jesus Christ as God, the second view makes him appear but as man. Furthermore, the supernaturalistic picture of the miraculous intervention of the otherworldly God at a certain point in the course of history does not permit a plausible answer to the question of how the benefit of this divine act can be transferred to the present; and the evolutionistic philosophy which claims to observe in Jesus the appearance of a divine *principle* (*e.g.* the power which governs the universe is love; the nobility of human life consists in forgiving and serving; each human soul is of infinite value, *etc.*) cannot make plain why one should *bind* the present, which acknowledges the validity of this principle, to an event or a person of the past.

It is Barth's distinction that he clearly recognizes the weight of the problem of revelation. His emphasis on the transcendence of God is noteworthy. It gives recognition to the almost inexpressible, but genuine tendency of the religious faith to devote itself to something that is unseen and yet hoped for, unrealized and yet real. The God of a true religion is always a god who is not attained. He is worshiped as the absolute "More," "Not-Yet," "Yonder," and this "More," "Not-Yet," "Yonder" is related to human life in pious adoration, veneration and devotion. Barth's emphasis on this transcendence is the result of his appreciation of the true *form* of the religious attitude. We must ask, however, whether he has succeeded in filling this form with particularly Christian content, whether he has made it convincingly authoritative by linking it to Jesus Christ. We must ask whether his theology states and adequately explains that God has revealed himself in Jesus Christ or whether it only points out what *revelation ought to be.* Is his theology based on the "Christian revelation," or is it a *speculation on revelation,* which happens to employ Christian material?

Some light will be thrown on these questions by further attention to Barth's theological conclusions. In § 7 of the *Dogmatics,* he deals with the important problems, how the reality of the Word of God—we may also say, the reality of *God*—can be known. Here he brings out the characteristics of his thought, and, in many respects, offers the key to his entire theology.

He begins the discussion with a description of the theme of dogmatics as it is understood by modern Protestant theologians. "According to the unanimous and clear opinion of Neo-Protestant teachers, the topic of dogmatics is the Christian *religion*, the Christian *consciousness*, the Christian *faith* (more often even the Christian faith as modified by *contemporary* thought); the object of this faith, however, is the topic of dogmatics only in so far as it is taken as the *expression*, or to speak with Wobbermin, as the *object-content* of faith." [10] In strict contrast to this view, Barth identifies himself with the saying of Luther in the Smalkaldian articles (II, 2): *Verbum Dei condat articulos fidei et praeterea nemo, ne angelus quidem.* "The meaning and the possibility, the theme, of dogmatics is therefore not Christian faith, but the Word of God. For the Word of God is not founded upon Christian faith, but Christian faith is founded upon the word of God." [11]

...The objectivity of the Word of God and not subjective belief is the starting-point of theological labor. The term "Word of God," as it is here used, does not directly correspond with the "Biblical word," but rather with the "revelation of God." Hence Barth's statement is even more startling. Does he intend to disregard the correlation between faith and revelation, upon which the power and persuasiveness of Protestant Christianity rests? Can he deny that many of the most convincing statements of Luther depend upon his understanding faith as trust (*fiducia*) and that, therefore, the essence of evangelical Christianity is belief in God in whom one can absolutely trust? Of course he cannot. But he declares that the word *fiducia* has not only this "emotional" but also a juristic meaning. It may refer, he says, to a contract for a concession to a property, or the security received in such a transaction. *Fiducia* takes place as a response to the act or word of another, from whom one has received a deposit. Applied to the religious field, faith is, therefore, that human attitude or act which is the only possible way of recognizing that God has addressed himself to man. It is an *answer*.[12] The theme of dogmatics is, therefore, the Word of God, the objectivity of the divine revelation, and not faith and its content.

What knowledge may we have of the reality of the "Word of God"? Can we know any reality except as it is the content of our own consciousness? The revelation of God, when it becomes knowable to us, would appear necessarily to be *reality in our consciousness.* "We are here—together with the modern theologians —face to face with the full weight of the axiom that reality is knowable only as reality-in-consciousness. We have to deal with the question of how we can know the reality of the "Word of God," if we refuse to understand it, as "object-content" of faith. Do we perhaps find it by submission to an authority? Or have we some speculation in mind by which we might prove *in* consciousness a yonder of consciousness? Or can we claim to be participants in a special view of reality—a view to be made intelligible, perhaps, by parapsychology? Even then we would explain it as a reality of consciousness, though an extraordinary one. And if we do not mean it so, what else can we do but turn back to the broad theological highway, where, as every reasonable person knows, what we called the "Word of God," is given in faith—*i.e.*, as object-content of faith

and therefore of human consciousness. A turning
back to that highway, however, cannot be considered,
for we would be unable to take along what we have
discovered as the concept of the Word of God. We
have found that the Word of God is to be understood
as the speech of God, an act the subject of which is
God and God alone. As such, this reality can evidently
not be part of the content of our human consciousness.
It is real only in the consciousness of God. As such it
may be believed in faith, but not as if it were given to
man as the objective content of his faith. Faith believes
it precisely as that which is not given for man, but
belongs to God alone." [18] God is subject, not object.

How, then, can this subject be known? Barth answers: since there is nothing that can be superior to
the Word of God, the knowledge of its reality must
rest in itself. It must make itself known. Knowledge,
cognition of it, is, therefore, principally recognition.
"We do not know the word of God by and in ourselves,
but we know it by God and in God." Or, in other
words, we do not *know* it, but are known by it. God's
is the initiative.

For the moment, all this sounds acceptable. In such
a way Paul used to speak. Barth refers to him specifically. But Paul could say that he *was* known, because
he was sure of God's revelation in Jesus Christ, and this
certainly was guaranteed to him by the historical fact
of Jesus Christ and by faith. Was this faith of his nothing but receptivity, vacuum, to be filled by the disclosure of God, or was it a peculiar inner attitude and
perspective by which he was enabled to see what ordinary, unbelieving eyes could not?

What enables me to become aware of something,
otherwise unknown to me, must be more than a re-

ceptacle to be filled. Faith is, therefore, a creative as well as a responsive faculty; and Barth's understanding of it cannot be considered adequate. He would probably answer that the creative quality of faith, if it does exist, is not a natural property of man, but the gift of the Holy Spirit. We would then ask him to explain how he could possibly know that this Holy Spirit is given from above, and the answer would have to affirm either that there is in human consciousness an inherent faculty which enables us to distinguish between the human and the divine or that God gives this knowledge. This second answer would simply be a return of our question. Our question would then be answered by a question. Barth decides, indeed, for this possibility. He does not deny that his theory of the knowledge of the word of God has the logical form of a *petitio principii.* He says: "How do you know the Word of God? I answer: by having known it before I knew of it and by the fact that God has spoken it to me." [14]

Here again it is evident that Barth is perilously near the conception of idealistic philosophy to which he objects so strenuously. If he declares that he has known the Word of God before he came to know it, he makes a statement which seems to presuppose an *a priori* antecedent of that which was to be known. He avoids this interpretation only because he operates with the postulates that God is transcendent and that God's is the initiative. But these postulates are a matter of faith. Barth seems to be engaged in a vain struggle against windmills.

Is he really? Does he really return to a position against which he intends to launch his weighty arguments? No; he does not. The faith which must be

ascribed to him and which he does not hesitate to defend is not a *creative* religious attitude, in which God
is immanent. He himself defines it by the words
"obedience," and "recognition." But this conception
of faith is the reflection of a concept of God, which is
not fully clear in itself. It is made up of two elements:
The first is an affirmation of the transcendence of God.
By this he deprives himself of the possibility of making
a positive statement about God. He is thereby in a position to say what God is *not,* and on this basis he can
criticize any human attitude which claims immediacy
with the divine. The second is characterized by his
constant repetition that God is subject, acting subject,
that *he* makes the beginning, and that *he* takes the
initiative. He must have in mind a conception of God
equal or at least similar to that of a supernatural being,
who has disclosed himself in a miraculous fashion at a
certain point in history or as an absolute personality
whose acts must be obediently accepted. The term
"Word of God" symbolizes the strange togetherness
of these two concepts. When he puts the emphasis
upon "God," he contrasts the "Word of *God,*" with
the word of man, thereby asserting the transcendence
of the divine. When he stresses the "Word of God" as
a whole, he seems to refer to the authority of the Scrip-
tures or of Jesus Christ (in harmony with the gospel
of John and its interpretation of Jesus as Logos—
Word).

We arrive, therefore, at the conclusion that Barth
avoids a return to the theological highway only because he keeps himself constantly aware of the transcendence of God, of the infinite, qualitative difference and between time and eternity. The logic of *this*
emphasis would lead him, of course, to a point where

he would be incapable even of speaking of God, where he could only say *that*, but under no circumstances *what* God is, not even that he is a subject. *That* is possible for him only because he accepts the Christian or at least the Biblical tradition. But the testimony of the Apostles, without which, as we have heard, no preaching would take place, is certainly an expression of faith, of a faith which is more than obedience. If it is the recognition of an event which is describable as the revelation of God, it is certainly either an interpreting recognition or the acceptance of an authority. We must remember, of course, that Barth wishes to avoid this understanding of the apostolic tradition. He tells us to distinguish in the *"Paulus dixit"* the *"Deus dixit,"* to see behind the Biblical word the immediate revelation of God, who is subject, the totally other subject. He applies thus also to the Bible the dialectical crisis which results from the concept of a transcendent God. However, all this in no way obscures the fact that the Christian's knowledge of God ultimately depends on faith in the Apostles—*i.e.*, on the trust in their interpreting testimony. If pressed so far, Barth would have to admit that the authority by which one arrives at the reality of the Word of God is a human attitude.

The result of our analysis can now be summed up.

God is unknown, because he is absolutely transcendent. This is a critical theological idea which expresses in *utmost* radicalness the conviction of the Idealists (and of many modern theologians since Schleiermacher), that God cannot be "something given."

Faith in God is a daring venture, which cannot be supported by any of the proofs which otherwise sustain and underlie human enterprises. Unashamed the believer must take his chances with God alone, obediently surrendering himself to God, hoping that *he* will make *himself* known. It must be said more especially of the Christian that he must, without shame, take his chances with the testimony of the men of the Bible.

The abstractness of these thoughts is obvious. Even in regard to the Christian "tradition," Barth cannot avoid abstractness. He finally pleads for "pure doctrine." He attempts, however, to counteract this impression by calling attention to the fact that no man can think these thoughts without realizing that they concern very concretely *his own existence*, that he is involved in them not as a spectator, but as an actor. He *lives* the conflicts which are aroused when the word "God" is uttered.

It will perhaps be helpful to introduce at this point a lecture on "Fate and Idea in Theology" which Barth delivered in 1929.[15] In it he deals with the problems of reality and truth, Realism and Idealism, with which the philosophers struggle when they wish to interpret the fundamental principles of human existence. We have seen that Barth was unable to avoid reference to these problems when he had to explain the underlying attitude of his thinking. In this lecture, he faces frankly the issues. Theology, he declares, is the science of God as he is preached in the church. As such it is a human science, involved, therefore, in the same fundamental problems with which the philosophers have to concern themselves. God and reality, God and truth—these are the themes to which he addresses himself. His conclusions will help us to evaluate the main tendencies of his theology.

"God is reality." There can be no doubt that theology cannot dispense with the concept of a given reality. "God is"—that is a fundamental sentence of all theology. The Realist must necessarily think of God in the same manner that he thinks of himself and of things. For if God is, he must be part of being, and being is both within and without. God, the theological Realist concludes, is, therefore given inwardly and outwardly, in subjective and in objective experience. He is in the universe and in our feelings—as Schleiermacher taught. Barth prefers to say that he is that reality by which the actuality of ourselves and of our world *becomes* real. He is the reality of all realities, that which constitutes them as actual.

But as such God is not a hidden element of reality. He is not "fate," something given in consciousness or in the outer world. It is just here that theology differs from philosophy, for it relates itself to the revelation of God, in which God is revealed as well as concealed. He is not given unless he gives himself. Knowledge of God is always grace, grace to sinners—*i.e.*, to men who have no knowledge of God in themselves; it must be bestowed upon them. If it were true that God is directly given to us, should he then not better be called "nature"? And should one then not speak of *demon*ology rather than *the*ology? Barth comes to the conclusion that a God who is Nature would not be the God who has revealed himself in his Word.

"God is truth." Who could deny that theology must employ the attitude of the Idealist! All idealistic thinking is engaged in a search for something superior to reality, something that as unconditioned, unobjective, ungiven, is conditioning reality. It asks for something that is higher than the correlation of subject and object. It attempts to assert spirit against nature. No theology can avoid following in the steps of Ideal-

ism, if it thinks about God. Even realistic theology
cannot do without heavy borrowings from Idealism.
Whenever the idea of God is contemplated seriously,
the way in which *he* is given must be strictly distinguished from that in which everything else is given.
The difference is so great that in comparison to all
other kinds of existence or being, one must speak of
the non-existence, the non-givenness of God. Theology must therefore necessarily be as idealistic as it
must be realistic. "Consideration of the reality of God
involves always a transcending of this reality in the
direction of its truth, which is not given."

All reservations made in regard to the realistic concepts of God, seem to be rooted in the truth of Idealism. God is not fate. God is not nature. The word became flesh; but the flesh in itself is not the word, except in so far as the *word* became flesh. One cannot
say that these limitations are clearly safeguarded in the
presuppositions of theological Realism. Even the concealment of God in revelation is evidently the interest
of Idealism in theology. It proclaims "God is truth"
over against "God is reality," as the Realists say. It does
not deny reality, but wants to consider it transparent,
so that truth may shine through it—truth, without
which it would not be the reality of God. This is why it
criticizes objective as well as subjective experience,
and is the reason why it speaks—to the displeasure of
the Realists—of the symbolical character of the subjective and objective givenness of God. Idealism protects theology against the possibility of making God
identical with or equal to objects or things. "Idealism
directs theological thinking toward that God who is
really God only in his transcendence (*Jenseitigkeit*),"

Idealism saves theology from becoming demonology. In this it proves its necessity. After Barth has thus affirmed the *raison d'être* of Idealism in theological thought, he proceeds to qualify this affirmation by certain doubting questions: He points out that Christian thought claims to be dependent upon revelation. This is to say that God can be conceived as truth not because critical thinking has led man to such a conception, but because God himself has made the conception possible. He asks the idealistic theologian whether the "Yonder" of God, which he stresses, is "a yonder of our own created and fallen spirit, the relative invisibility of our own spiritual life," or whether it is the "Yonder of the Creator of heaven and earth, of nature and the spirit, *visibilium omnium et invisibilium.*" Only the second possibility is acceptable to theology, since "it is the science of the Word of that God who lives in a light no man can approach unto." All this means that the knowledge of the truth of God is not the result of an act of man, but only of God. Cognition of God can be but recognition of God. If Idealism leads theology to the equation God = reason (ratio), it must be rejected no less definitely than Realism, which proposes the equation God = nature. Ideology is just as intolerable to theology as demonology, for faith believes in a God who is superior both to nature and reason (or spirit).

God is true reality and real truth. Theology must, therefore, think in terms of Realism *and* Idealism. Are we then to assume that it achieves the synthesis by contrasting reality and truth? If that were so, it would not fundamentally differ from philosophy. All philosophers must find means of establishing a *tertium,* a harmony which binds together the genuine and incontrovertible interests of Realism and Idealism. Is theology then a special type of philosophy, in so far as it comes to the conclusion that in God this synthesis is reached? Barth very significantly answers that the *tertium*, the unity between reality and truth, which man might claim to have found by way of venturesome and courageous speculation, is not God. *This* "Totally Other" is but a reflection of man, his own image, "a final stone in the vault of his art," the last, the highest of his works. *This* "other" is still only *his* other, not the Totally Other. This concept of God is the philosopher's, the theosophists, not the concept of the theologian. It is a *thought* of the synthesis, but not the synthesis itself.

The real and true synthesis cannot be known by man: it can only be believed. He cannot create: he can only receive it. He cannot go *to* it, but only come *from* it. *I* cannot find God, but he must find *me*. No true theology can, therefore, avoid the idea of predestination and election. It is God himself who grants the belief, thus making himself known. And belief will obediently submit to the revelation in Jesus Christ, where the Word of God has become flesh, disclosing itself as the true reality and real truth.

At first hearing, all this sounds plausible, but the old difficulties recur.

The conflict between Realism and Idealism is acute in every mind troubled by the desire for the understanding of life. If it could be dissolved, we would be freed from one of the most pressing intellectual problems. When men seek God, in whom the meaning of life rests, they are engaged in the search for the synthesis of truth and reality. It is plain that the only adequate concept of God is one which holds truth and reality together. In so far as Barth demonstrates this fact we must be in hearty agreement with him.

We can follow him when he points out that the philosopher always moves toward this concept of God, ending his speculation however at this point, while the theologian begins with it, making it the basis of all his consideration of human life. Where the philosopher's *speculation ends,* the theologian's *belief begins.*

It is also clear that this belief or faith is devoted to something that is not given. The togetherness of truth and reality, of supreme value and fact, is not an attainment. If it were so, it would not have to be believed. The believer, therefore, will discover himself again and again as a "sinner." He must always begin anew and *hope* to realize what he knows to be God, the real truth and true reality, the fact full of supreme value and supreme value become fact. Hence God is yonder, never here. He remains the Totally Other. And because he remains so, he causes a crisis, a break-up in man; for man must come to the insight that in actual living he is not like God. Nor can he claim to have an inborn knowledge of God. He believes in God, however, and in believing he has God, but outside of his natural self, so to speak; he has the "Holy Spirit." Whenever man suffers himself to be broken by belief in God, he is blessed by the Holy Spirit. This, too, we can now understand. Faith depends really on more than an *a priori* antecedent within the human mind, and on more than an antecedent of fact, which can be experienced *a posteriori.* It is devotion to that truth-reality which no one of us can claim now to have, but from which we always come and toward which we continuously go.

In all this the genuine quality of the religious idea of revelation is adequately and admirably preserved. Devotion to this synthesis of truth and reality, which is truly the absolute "More," "Not Yet," "Yonder," is indeed identical with the idea of revelation, identical with faith in the disclosure of what is concealed. We cannot deny that the Christian tradition has many traces of it. The faith of the men of the Bible was of this *kind*. We can accept this conception of the revelation as an adequate interpretation of the *meaning* of the Johannine saying: "The word became flesh." We can even admit that it is a good definition of the *meaning* of the ancient Logos-Christology. *But* can it be called Christian in the sense that it is true only because it is found in the Christian tradition? and furthermore, is this revelation exclusively dependent upon Jesus Christ and the testimony of the Apostles concerning him?

Barth expects us to follow him when he answers this question in the affirmative. But that we cannot do. We do not feel any hestitation in declaring that he is probably right when he claims that his thinking is in accordance with the Biblical attitude; yet we cannot agree with him when, in consequence of these conclusions, he attempts to set up the Bible as the authority for the validity of this thinking. Of course we are aware that he qualifies his appeal to Biblical authority. He urges us to submit to it not because the church in its tradition has held it the sufficient norm of its preaching, and not because the Apostles have deposited in it their testimony, but because both church and Apostles refer back to the immediate revelation of God, of which they considered themselves witnesses. When Barth makes an appeal for social solidarity, calling our attention to the fact that as believers we depend upon the belief of our fathers, we are naturally willing to listen to him. What good fortune it would be, if we were convinced that the faith in which we feel we must live was essentially that of our ancestors! But surely our faith is not true because it is derived from theirs, but because it corresponds to the actual conditions under which we live. We accept their faith as true only if we feel that it agrees with our necessities. We gladly avail ourselves of the benefit of their experience. We might then even regard their testimony as a norm for our thinking and believing. In other words, their God is our God because we have discovered him as true, not because he was their God. We are obedient not to them, but to the truth of God; and our only authority is our own venturesome faith as we have been led to it by a sincere, open-minded consideration of the facts of life. God has revealed himself to us in the present life we are living. We believe in him because the realities of life compel us to. In these realities, he finds us. In this sense faith comes to us; we do not create it.

Our impression is that the ultimate authority on which Barth depends is no other than this, and we cannot avoid the conclusion that he is guilty of a strange self-deception, when he insists on pointing to the immediate revelation of God which is concealed in the Biblical testimony on Jesus Christ. He operates with a conception of revelation which is antiquated, outlived, unreal. It is the old supernaturalism, the old belief in the miraculous intervention of an otherworldly, superhuman, anthropomorphic God which haunts him.

It is not difficult to find the cause of this self-deception. In the experiences of the war he was forced to rethink his philosophy of life. The "infinite contradictions of human existence" which then overpowered him and which were brought close to him every Sunday by the people who filled the pews in the church where he preached, demanded absolute honesty. These contradictions could not be resolved by any sort of ideology, by any optimistic "Nevertheless." During that period, the Bible served as a guide to a new analysis of life. Its call to repentance, to a change of mind, its theology of the cross, of the broken spirit and the contrite heart, strangely coincided with the mood of post-war disillusionment. In the face of the facts which unveiled human life in its nakedness, a theology of the glory of man could not be recommended. The Bible seemed restored to its real significance, when, under these circumstances, it was presented as the gospel of the eschatological glory of God, unattainable except by men who, in frank consciousness of their unworthiness, did not cease to love the divine in the Holy Otherness of its unity of truth and reality, because they knew that the harmony of fact and value must underlie all existence, if the striving for its meaningfulness is to be judged as a response to an actuality and not as the vain pursuit of an absurd phantom. The terms of the Bible and the quaint concepts of traditional Christianity corresponded to this view of human life in its relation with God. They thus regained their validity. Gradually they became again authoritative and with them those factors which, in former times, had made them normative.

As a matter of fact, however, the Bible or traditional Christianity did not *cause* the awakening. They were only freshly appreciated because they were found to speak the truth about human life, when it stands face to face with that transcendental ground of all existence which, following Barth, we have just described as truth-reality, and which all believing mankind designates by the word "God." In other words, the modern Christian religion assumed a new meaning under the impact of the radically changed human situation of war and post-war days, and it appeared to be in accord with the general tendency of the Bible. But the recovery of the *meaning* of the Christian religion is not necessarily identical with the recovery of the *facts,* upon which according to old tradition and belief, it is built. A new understanding of the significance of the idea of revelation does not necessarily imply an acceptance of the so-called facts of revelation. That, however, is evidently Barth's conclusion. He seems to theologize on the basis of the *fact* that God has revealed himself in Jesus Christ, once for all. Rather uncritically he seems to accept this fact and with it much of the religious attitude without which it could not be accepted as a fact. We are aware that he qualifies all this very definitely by statements which are borne out by his own understanding of the *meaning.* When we consider his interpretation of the resurrection, for example, we find that he describes it first of all as a fact, but immediately informs us also that it is an *unhistorical* fact, which must in no way be put in line with other ordinary or extraordinary "events." The term "unhistorical fact" is absurd in the eyes of any one who is not acquainted with the complexity of Barthian thinking. It is supposed to carry two connotations: one which refers to the *meaning* for which the resurrection, *following* the *death* of Christ, stands; and another which simply deals with the *fact* of the resurrection. In a similar way, he seems to move from a concept of God which is in line with the old belief in a supernatural being miraculously intervening in the course of the world, to another which does justice to the *meaning* of this sort of faith. There is a vast difference between the concept of a sovereign God who *acts* upon the life of the world, and the concept of a God who is characterized as "Origin" or "Truth-reality"; but Barth does not seem to distinguish carefully enough between them.

Would it not be correct to describe the Barthian thought in the following way: it is a Christian *philosophy* of religion, in which early-Christian, Protestant and idealistic elements are combined? Early-Christian in its emphasis upon Eschatology, the trend toward the otherworldly, the coming glory of God; Protestant in its critical attitude toward life, its tendency to measure everything by the standard of divine fulfilment and supreme perfectness; idealistic in its stress upon the ungivenness of God. Under the influence of the two other factors, this non-objectivity of God is defined as absolute transcendence.

It is a philosophy which could originate only on Christian soil. It preserves the essential features of religion, in so far as life is linked to a transcending "value," which can be known only by belief in its "revelation," and the characteristic elements of Christianity, in so far as life is surveyed under the aspects of a repentant and renewing restlessness, which results from the fact that it is seen in relation to "God," whom the Christians significantly define as "Creator" and "Redeemer." No one who has ever struggled with the painful problem of the meaning of life, can doubt that God "is," and he is fully aware of the fact that God's "being" is totally different from that of any other mode of existence. No concept of God will, therefore, adequately describe God. It can be no more than symbol and parable. No one can justly "speak" of God nor rightfully claim to have God, albeit no one can afford to live without him.

Barth desires to inject all of these qualities of religious faith into our chaotic modern life; and few will be able to evade the deep emotional appeal which he makes. *He does it as a Christian preacher, as a minister of the "Reformed Church."* As such he relies on the tradition and the cultic forms with which his church provides him. He depends primarily on the Bible. Sermons on Biblical texts must carry his message. He finds that the *meaning* of the words of the Testaments is valid even today. He succeeds, therefore, in making the wall of twenty centuries transparent; Jeremiah and Paul speak to the Twentieth Century; the life and death of Jesus Christ become again the test and demonstration of "what God does to the world." He is conscious of the difference between Biblical thinking and the modern world-view. He observes in the Bible a dependence upon "primitive" environment and upon outlived historical conditions. He does not overlook its inadequacy of thought-forms and concepts. He professes, however, to be concerned only with the "Word in the words," with the ineffable, untouchable, eternal of which these words bear testimony. He is in search of the eternal truth.

Is he strong enough to live up to the full universality of this attitude? He remains the Protestant preacher and theologian. His philosophy of religion becomes a theology, an ecclesiastical theology. The Bible is his final authority after all. It alone is the instrument of salvation. God is confined to the words of the Biblical witnesses. The revelation took place in

"Palestine, A.D. 1-30," once, in Jesus Christ. *Deus dixit,* God *has* spoken.

The Barthian thought, richly endowed with a vital message for our groping time, full of the promise that it will give our religious needs new direction and new fulfilment, if it were concretely applied to them, assumes the appearance of another theological system, devoted to a re-interpretation of the dogmatic formulae which have been developed in the course of Christian history. A wide, Christian philosophy of religion of universal potentialities is returned to the narrow channels of ecclesiastical tradition. A vigorous plant, grown on the soil of the Christian civilization of the Twentieth Century, is not permitted to blossom because it is cultivated on the barren, exhausted field of theological scholasticism.

The strange complexity of Barth's theology is due to the fact that he insists on expressing the *meaning* of the Christian religion, which he has newly understood, in terms of an outworn theological tradition; and in the course of this procedure he often forgets that the recovery of the *meaning* of an old religious or theological concept does not need to coincide with the recovery of the concept itself, for that would lead to the adoption of thought-forms and beliefs which do not correspond to the facts as *we* know them.

This observation may be expressed in another way: Barth's theological ideas are the result of two different approaches. He himself defines them as the phenomenological and existential methods. They are applied in general to the same field, namely, to the field of man's relationship with God. But as a matter of fact, they lead to a discussion of subjects which are by no means identical. For the so-called *existential method* deals with the *life of man* in his unredeemed nature, qualified by the conflicts which point to the "otherness" of God. It reveals the crisis of human life which becomes apparent when man relates himself to the transcendent One, who is the synthesis of the conflicts of his existence, and without whom he cannot live— so that, in repentant, self-denying faith, he must constantly seek him in his supreme "otherness." It is apparent that this religious philosophy of life bears the mark of its Christian origin, as has been pointed out.

The *phenomenological method* deals with the fact that preaching is going on, which, according to Barth, is as certain a fact as rain. It investigates the truth of the Christian character of the sermons that are preached in the Christian churches. It presupposes, therefore, a definite *preaching tradition*, which, Barth believes, is rooted in the Biblical testimony of the apostles and prophets as to the revelation of God in Jesus Christ. *In this second phase of Barthian thinking, the entire tradition of the church, in so far as, in its message, it depends on the significance of Christ's appearance in the world, is taken for granted.*

The complexity of Barth's theology is due to his efforts to fuse these two methods and their respective material. He measures the truth of Christian preaching by the norm of the crisis between God and man, which he has derived from the "existential method." But the notion of this "crisis" is the result not only of an anlysis of life as such, but of the *Christian* life; its definitely Christian origin cannot be concealed. No one is more eager than Barth to point out its similarity to, if not identity with, the "Biblical attitude." The result of the correlation of these two methods is that Barth must make seemingly contradic-

tory statements about one and the same fact. When
he deals with Christian preaching, he must ask at
once, *how can* it be done? how *can* man speak of the
"totally other" God? When, in accordance with the
general Christian belief, he refers to God's revelation
in Jesus Christ, he must add at once the warning that
such a revelation cannot be other than that of the
hidden God. When he discusses the actual existence
of Christianity or of the church, he must explain at
once that, strictly speaking, Christianity *cannot* exist; for the Christian life is never more than an *eschatological* fact. The "infinite qualitative difference
between time and eternity," due to the observation
that "God is in heaven and man on earth" is kept in
mind in a thorough-going fashion. This principle is
not only critically applied to *modern* theology, but to
all Christian theology. The result is not only that any
sort of experience of God is rejected but also any *fact*
of divine revelation.

It seems at times, therefore, that the existential
method, ending in the theology of crisis, controls the
thought of Barth. It appears also that the review of
Christian theology under the aspect of the "crisis" is
largely a waste of effort. How much more valuable it
would be, if Barth would pay more attention to the
problems of contemporary life, if he would tell his
fellow men what should be done in view of the situation in which they find themselves, or if he would at
least unfold the *ethos* which would express devotion
to the supreme God who torments us because in him
the conflicts of our lives take shape, yet without whom
we cannot live.

Barth, however, is not conscious of *reviewing* Christian theology under the aspect of the "crisis." He

claims adequately to present a Christian theology on the basis of the *fact* that God has revealed himself in Jesus Christ, as the creeds of the church confess. The phenomenological method thus seems at times to supersede the existential one.

Barth does not wish to be a philosopher, but a theologian. Nevertheless, he is in reality a philosopher of the meaning of life, who attempts to avoid the reproach of subjectivism and arbitrariness which such a philosopher has to expect, by entrenching himself in the authority of Christian tradition, of Biblical testimony, and even of the revelation of God himself. In the objectivity of the "Word" his thought is seemingly made secure.

VII

BARTHIANISM AS A NEW THEOLOGY:

THE DOGMATIC SYSTEM

THE foregoing will be made plain as we devote ourselves to a brief discussion of the distinctly dogmatic chapters of the *Prolegomena*. They are entitled: The revelation of God; the Holy Scripture; the Message of the Church. We will observe a continuous shifting from revelation as a crisis (God, in whom the meaning of life is guaranteed, being transcendent) to revelation as a fact (in Jesus Christ), and a constant dialectical correlation of these two concepts.

According to Barth, the revelation of God is identical with the "Word of God." He paraphrases this latter concept by the sentence "God speaks—*Deus dixit*." [1] Inadvertently, he illustrates in these few words the contradictory character of his entire endeavor. When he describes the divine revelation by saying "God *speaks*," (present tense) he wishes to emphasize the fact that we can conceive of a revelation only by acknowledging that *God* and not man is its subject. Recognition of the divine transcendence is identical with the belief in the divine revelation.

Barth adds to this another sentence, *Deus dixit*, "God *has* spoken," (past tense). Thereby he refers to the revelation in Jesus Christ, of which the Apostles

174

are said to be witnesses. He thus accepts the theological
tradition of the Church, and gives expression to his
intention "to place himself as a thinker in the church,
into whose faith he was baptized", and "to do his
thinking on the basis of the Biblical testimony of the
revelation," [2] on the basis of the believed *fact* that
Jesus Christ is Lord—*i.e.*, the revealer of God.

If asked what this thinking would be, Barth would
answer that it must be determined by the awareness
of God's transcendence, which is to say that it must
be dialectical thinking. He thus applies his religious
philosophy of life—derived from the observation that
life is unredeemed, full of conflict, not God-like, never
realizing the supreme value (truth-reality) *etc.*—as a
method of thinking to the theological tradition of
the church which is as uncritically accepted as if it
were a necessity. As a matter of fact, the only necessity
for accepting tradition is Barth's own desire to be a
good theologian, or at least a good member of the
church. In consequence, we can never be certain
whether he intends to illustrate his religious philosophy of life by the use of the material of traditional
Christian theology, or whether the understanding of
the theology of the church is his primary concern.

It would seem that a decision about this problem
might be very simply reached; for the *Dogmatics* presents a full discussion of the old theological concepts,
foremost among which is the doctrine of the Trinity.
It would appear, therefore, that Barth were really
primarily interested in the dogma of the church. But
immediately, in the beginning of the discussion of the
trinitarian doctrine, he makes us doubt whether we
can adhere to this assumption. He does not set out
with the historical observation that the early Chris-

tian belief in Jesus Christ as the revelation of God had necessarily to follow in a speculation on the connection between the Son and the Father, particularly if the Jewish monotheism were to be retained, but he starts with a logical explanation of the sentence "God speaks." He inquires [3] for its subject, predicate, and object. "We ask, Who speaks?" and answer "the Lord!," —therefore he alone is the revealer. "We go on to ask, What happens here? and answer, "The Lord *speaks*." That must mean, he is wholly revelation." We ask finally "what is here spoken and revealed?" and answer, "The Lord declares that he is Lord, *i.e.* he himself is that which is revealed." Thus God himself is subject, predicate and object of the sentence, God speaks. God alone, he himself exclusively, is the revealer; he alone is the agent of revelation, and he alone its content. How could the absolute subjectivity of God be more definitely affirmed? How could his absolute transcendence, his incomprehensibility be more drastically expressed? All this is nothing but a speculation, a logical, even grammatical construction, which is supposed strictly to safeguard the idea that God is God—in himself, to himself, by himself.

It must, of course, be admitted that the trinitarian dogma is built upon this very idea. Barth is, therefore, seemingly justified when he applies his construction to the theological tradition of the church. No one who is acquainted with the historical development of the doctrine of the Trinity will deny that the Fathers of the church were guided by other interests than Barth's. Moreover, even if it were true that the trinitarian doctrine presented, with indubitable clarity, a concept of the absolute lordship of God who "confronts man as an indissoluble subject," it is difficult to see why a theologian of the Twentieth Century should busy himself with such a complicated, almost unintelligible reconstruction of it as Barth attempts to achieve. If he undertook it for the sake of historical understanding, one would be willing to follow him, but he obviously does not desire to be considered a historian. He is thinking on the basis of the apostolic confession that Jesus Christ is Lord, κύϱιος, *i.e.* God.

It cannot be denied that the ancient church was forced into the Christological and trinitarian controversies because it accepted this belief of the Apostles. Barth explains his own interest in the Trinity on the same ground. But the difference between his view and the traditional theological one is, that the founders of the trinitarian dogma were chiefly concerned with the proof that the one living God, who according to the Old Testament had created the world and governed it, had really revealed himself as the Redeemer in Jesus Christ; while Barth is primarily interested in showing that God who, in order to be God must be conceived as the transcendent One, remains such even if he has revealed himself in Jesus Christ. The ancient theologians believed in Christ, because they saw in him the divine Saviour, and felt compelled to prove his identity with the supreme God and ruler of the world. All their theological speculations were dominated by a definite sense of salvation from sin. They were built up, not without definite indebtedness to Paul, in a great religious philosophy of a supernatural drama of fall and redemption compassing the whole universe from the beginning to the end of time. The effectiveness of this drama depended upon the trinity of Father, Son, and Holy Spirit (Creator, Saviour, Redeemer). It is highly significant to observe that Barth, in his theology, disregards this ancient idea of salvation, at least its particular content. It is equally strange that he does not feel the need of including the problem of "sin" in his discussion. Consequently, he cannot possibly be in accord with the ancient fathers, even if he claims to think on the basis of their belief. In reality, *he* believes something else. It may be misleading to say that Barth substitutes for the ancient idea of salvation the idea of the recognition of the transcendence of God and that he puts the "brokenness," the "infinite contradiction" in the life of man in the place of sin. Inadequate as such a statement may be, it probably suggests in an accurate way what has taken place. For there can be no doubt that Barth's trinitarian discussion is unconvincing to a theologian versed in the history of dogma because he lays the emphasis exclusively upon the divine otherness.

If Barth accepted the trinitarian theology in its original design, and if, in his own exposition of it, he had stressed those phases of it which involve attention to the divine in contrast to the human, no objection could be raised against him; for these phases are certainly not lacking in ancient Orthodoxy as it defended itself against the heresies, notably Adoptianism and Arianism. It cannot be held, however, that Barth's theology is fundamentally of the same character as that of Athanasius, for example, for he surely does not base his thought upon the conviction that in Jesus Christ divine, immortal powers have entered the life of man, which if properly received through the service of the church, will assure man of an eternal, imperishable blessedness after, and in spite of physical death. Barth's understanding of Christianity does

not depend upon the certainty of a divine act of salvation. He does not presuppose the fact of an influx of
supernatural powers into the world. The positive content of the old theology is *not* to be found in his
thought.

He has taken over, however, its *form,* and occasionally he permits us to get glimpses of the content
which he would like to put into it. We hold that the
positive element of his thought is a religious philosophy of life, which surveys the conflicts of human
existence from the viewpoint of their transcendent
synthesis. Is that not something other than the drama
of salvation which the ancient church developed? It
may be its *meaning*—as we have suggested in another
connection—but it is certainly not the same in actual
development of content. Barth uses the old dogmatic
expressions, however, as if he were totally unaware
of the difference. God ' is the Creator—that is to say
he is the transcendent Lord above and beyond man's
contradiction over against God and within himself.
God is the Reconciler—that is to say he is the transcendent Lord who is victorious in the midst of man's
contradiction over against God and within himself.
God is Redeemer—that is to say he is the transcendent
Lord who dissolves man's contradiction over against
God and within himself. This is an artificial way of describing the fundamental thought of this theology:
man finds that his existence is not unified. It is full of
unsolved questions and contrasts. It is constantly confronted by the condemnation of meaninglessness. But
in the belief of God he is saved from this curse. God
is the answer to the question of his existence. In him
the conflicts are overcome, for he is that "order of
the universe" in which the unity of all its values is

constituted. Our devotion to him is, therefore, the expression of the conviction that the contradictions of our existence may be dissolved, in fact are dissolved, because life is conditioned by the unconditioned truth-reality. By submission to this transcendent "constitutor" of meaning, our lives may be qualitatively redeemed—in a continuous becoming, in a constant rebirth of faith in this God. The actual achievement of meaningful living is the *futurum resurrectionis*—the future of the resurrection, when we too will have "entered" the transcendent realm.

Someone may ask, if this is the content of Barth's message, why does he clothe it in the complicated system of Christian tradition; why must he relate his philosophy to Jesus Christ? The answer is that, although this is essentially Barth's thought, it is by no means all of it. For, in his eyes, God is ever more than the ground of the world, the unconditioned root of all existence; he is not the last that philosophy can say, but he is a person, who confrants man as *Thou*, therefore, as an indissoluble subject, as Thou, from which one cannot abstract, behind which neither being nor idea stand, and from which no effects emanate which are anything else than this Thou, this divine Thou, by which the human self is addressed as by its Lord. God is our God only in that he confronts us in no other way than as such a Thou. *Precisely* in this revelation, God discloses himself as the absolute Lord. "His revelation is, therefore, an event which does not occur everywhere. The life of the world, either as macrocosm or microcosm, is not the word of God. It is a particular, singular, incidentally contingent event, limited in space and time, a *hic et nunc* from the side of man who hears, an *illic et tunc,* from the side of

God who speaks. Here and now it is heard, because there and then it was spoken. It is not a mere symbol of the word of God, when Jesus Christ (years 1-30; Palestine) speaks to me here, today, but the fact that he does speak *is* the event of the word of God to the sinner." [5] God is the living God, the inexhaustible, absolute, indissoluble subject. He *acts*. As such he can be known, according to the Christian tradition, which Barth accepts, only in Jesus Christ.

These supernaturalistic elements in Barth's theology must not be overlooked. The gap between Athanasius and Barth is evidently not as deep as we supposed. God is not only the transcendent meaning-reality of our existence and as such its ground (or "origin"), he is also the supreme, supernatural personality. Divine revelation is, therefore, the eternal disclosure of the "totally other," unlimited by time or space, *and* it is the appearance of the living God at a definite point of history in a definite person. This latter concept is characteristic of Christian tradition. When Barth accepts it, he builds it into the first one, which fundamentally determines his thinking. He borrows, therefore, not only the form of Christian tradition, but with it also its definite content. And that is the chief reason for the often unintelligible complexity of his thinking.

"Jesus Christ, the Logos of God, the revelation, the Lord himself"—is the basis also of his doctrine of the trinity. How does he reconcile therein his two points of view? Let Barth himself give the answer. Jesus is Lord because he reveals the *Father*.

"All four gospels describe the life of Jesus as a history which, beginning swiftly and with ever increasing momentum, becomes the history of suffering and death. The suffering servant of Isaiah is rediscovered in Jesus (Act. VI, 26). Paul concerned himself nearly exclusively with Jesus and him crucified, and the author of the *Epistle to the Hebrews* saw in him the sacrifice of the new covenant between God and man. According to the New Testament the life of Jesus is the act of obedience 'unto death, even the death of the cross' (Phil. II, 8) ... Wherefore God also hath highly exalted him and given him a name which is above every name— 'Jesus Christ, the Lord,' (Phil. II, 9, 11); worthy is the Lamb that was slain to receive power, and riches, and wisdom, and strength, and honor, and glory, and blessing. (Rev. V, 12), ἐν τῇ ταπεινώσει ἡ κρίσις αὐτοῦ ἤρθη (Act. VIII, 33), (in his humiliation his judgment (crisis) was taken away); from *thence*, from an unheard of space beyond the *death* of the man Jesus of Nazareth that light is cast upon him which renders him the revelation of God, the Father. . . . Whom has a man in mind when he is compelled to call him who reveals himself in Jesus, 'Abba, Father?' (Rm. VIII, 15; Gal. IX, 6). Evidently the revelation in Jesus has taken all doubt from that man that he who is here revealed lives and has his being in a totally different sphere from man. The man to whom Jesus, in the service of the Father, reveals the Father (John XIV, 7), and—who, like the men of the Bible, hears through Jesus the word of God ... views himself and man in general as in contradiction to God. By this he sees himself drawn into the death of the man Jesus. . . . He is baptized in the name of Jesus and, in this baptism, his whole existence with all its contradictions, is caught into

the death of Jesus (Rm. VI, 3; Col. II, 12). With
Christ he is 'raised from the dead,' 'with him risen'
with him made to 'sit together in heavenly places'
(Col. II, 12; 3; Eph. II, 5). To hear the word of
God through Jesus, means the incomprehensible end
of our existence in contradiction; incomprehensible new beginning beyond this contradiction. The
word of God? What is it? Evidently the word of
him who is mighty enough to reconcile himself with
us, of him who stands *above* the contradiction in
which we find ourselves, *above* our contradiction
toward him and above our contradiction toward
ourselves. *Above* our contradiction and mighty
enough to reconcile us with him in order finally to
save us *from* our contradiction—evidently because
he is before our contradiction, because he is lord
over the contrasts of our existence in such a way
that they would not have come to be without him—
the Creator. . . . He proves himself the lord of our
life who orders in Jesus its death and resurrection.
. . . God as creator is the beginner of all that is real
outside of him, the beginner beyond all dialectic of
what is real outside of him, the One prior to and
above all twos that we cannot unite into one, even
above Creator and creature, as well as above the
divine holiness and our sin, the truth prior to and
above all truths, the home which man has left and
which still is his home; the Lord out of whom (ἐξοῦ)
are all things, whatever they may be to us, the
superior one to whom nobody and nothing is superior . . . God does not reveal himself without his
creation, but in and through it, and in such a way
that he alone is the revealer, he alone is Lord. God
is not revealed without his creation but he is re-

vealed as its creator *ex nihilo,* prior to it; and this
same God in this same way reveals himself in Jesus,
his servant. He is God the Father." [6]

God the Father and Creator is thus disclosed in
Jesus. But who is this Jesus in whom such a revelation
becomes real? This question Barth answers also by reference to the confession of the early Christian congregation: "Jesus, the Lord"—which is to say: he himself is God. But how can that be? Is he to be understood as the apotheosis of a man? Are we supposed to
believe, as some modern scholars would persuade us,
that out of pious veneration the disciples of Jesus gradually elevated him to the place of God—first a Gali-
lean Rabbi, then a prophet of the rank of an Elijah,
then a political, then a heavenly Messiah, then the Son
of God, and finally God himself? Or shall we assume,
that the docetic Christology is more accurate, which
sees in Jesus an appearance of the divine? The church
has refuted both Ebionitism and Docetism. The thesis
of the divinity of Christ has nothing to do with the
apotheosis of a man nor with the personification of
the divine within him. Neither theory adequately explains the thinking which finally ended in the belief
in the divinity of Jesus. How can one hold, Barth
asks, that a man ascended to the position of God or
that God descended upon a man, unless he has presupposed what he desires to prove by such theories?
For Barth at least it is a certainty that the early Christians *began* their preaching with the *axiom* that Jesus
was the Lord God, because only God can reveal God.
Finitum non capax infiniti. He who confesses a revelation of the Father, confesses—only an either—or being permitted—that he has seen one who is equal to

the Father, equal in his divinity, but *not* equal merely in that he is the Son of the Father.

But what is the meaning of the belief in the Son of God? "When man recognises the Lord not only as the 'Whence' of revelation, as the revealer, but also as the revelation itself, he comes to know the Lord not only *above,* but also *in* the contradiction of his existence. He meets him in the human realm. . . . Revelation occurs in spite of our contradiction toward God; for revelation places God in the midst of this our contradiction . . . God was in Christ and reconciled the world to himself, (II Cor. II, 13; Col. I, 13). . . . The boundlessness of our contradiction, the radicalness of our limitation, the "to and fro of the two worlds in which we move is *not*—as revelation discloses—without Logos, without God. God is not only the supreme Lord over all the world, but also the victorious Lord in all the world, not only as it was and will be, but also as it is, in sinfulness and perishableness." [7] In the Lord, God is the Reconciler.

Finally, we must ask, what man can receive through Jesus such a revelation? Who is he who can believe in the Father through the Son, and in the Son through the Father?

"Believing in supermen and demigods, in heroes and great personalities, in potencies, hypostases and mighty *ideas,* in deifications of nature and naturalisations of God—this has always been a possibility for man. *Finitum capax infiniti*—the whole history of religion is witness of it. But believing in God? This possibility did not appear as natural to the authors of the New Testament as to many of their modern readers. According to their unanimous testimony such a thing could become actual only through the Holy Spirit, through the 'activity' of a third principle of revelation." "It is not sufficient that God is Lord over our contradictions; neither does it suffice that he is Lord in the midst of our contradictions. For we are still outside of his lordship ... unless he is Lord in the suspension of our contradiction, unless the 'nevertheless' of his lordship applies to *us*. When we speak of the Holy Spirit, we are saying that we become participants of his superiority and his victory, that we become subject to his power as Creator and Reconciler." But "these sentences about the holy spirit and the effect of it must by no means be altered into sentences about man. They speak of God and his lordship, and not of man, neither of his nature nor of his spirit, neither of his heart nor of his conscience, ... neither of his knowing and willing nor of his feeling and experience. ... The work of God the Redeemer, who puts an end to our contradiction toward him and toward ourselves, is a real work, but one that is not yet fulfilled and completed in the man whom it touches. It is a work which is essentially to be fulfilled and achieved in the future." "In regard to man's relation with God the Redeemer, or God the spirit ... it must be said that everything that concerns man's part is pure hope; it is eschatology in the strictest sense of the word. ... God gives himself in his revelation in such a way that, though rich in him, we are and remain poor. A quantitative or qualitative ramification or development of man is *not* implied in the idea of the Holy Spirit; a new anthropology does not follow from it, however eagerly, in harmony with the Catholic doctrine of grace, the liberal and orthodox Neo-Protestants call for it.

Only as he is, does man receive the Holy Spirit; as he is, *i.e.* with totally empty hands, he comes into possession of the spirit. Descending upon all flesh, the holy spirit remains the *holy* spirit, through and through the spirit of what man shall *become*— and not of what he already *is*." " 'In the spirit' —we make confession of our absolute poverty, our broken conscience, our worldliness, our 'broken and contrite heart' (Ps. LI, 12). 'In the spirit' we know that we can only *pray* for a clean heart and a renewed right spirit within us, that what is born of the flesh is flesh (and this refers to our entire existence), and spirit is born of the spirit (John III, 6): the same existence, I, as I am, comprehended by and in God. . . . No limitation of the effect of the spirit is here affirmed, and no curtailment and no emptying of the God-relationship, no uncertainty of faith. Everything depends on this: that the God-relationship remain full of content and vitality, that faith stand on immovable ground, that this ground, this life, this truth be sought, not only in the first but also at the last and all the time, in God and nowhere else—and not within ourselves. Even the *received* Holy Spirit is grace." [8]

We have given these full quotations of Barth's own words in order to illustrate concretely the problem which we consider the most difficult one in his thinking. The reader can now judge for himself whether it is right to question Barth's acceptance of the Christian tradition.

What has just been outlined in the quoted passages is Barth's doctrine of the Trinity. It is clear that it is connected with the Christian church's traditional belief that God has revealed himself in Jesus Christ.

Barth does not, however, outline this belief in a historical review. No attempt is made to investigate how it originated, how it developed, and perhaps changed. He simply points out that the apostles confessed that Jesus Christ was Lord—*i.e.*, God. What they meant by such a testimony is explained by the use of a number of sayings of the Bible taken from its various parts; but a characterization and evaluation of these parts is nowhere given. Reference is made to numerous writers of the church universal and to the creeds. With a glorious air of definiteness and assurance, it is presupposed that these citations can have only one meaning, namely that allotted to them by Barth. He is seemingly absolutely certain of presenting the conviction of the authors of the New Testament and of ecclesiastical tradition. But one who is acquainted with the history of the thought of the church since its beginnings soon discovers that what Barth is really presenting is a new interpretation of certain of its phases—an interpretation not derived from a painstaking analysis of the original sources, but inspired by a point of view brought to them from outside. It is characterized first of all by Barth's conviction that the outlook of the men of the Bible, when they spoke of God, must have been the same as ours: God—then and now—is always God, and not man or the world. The qualitative difference between time and eternity must never be forgotten. God is the reality beyond all the realities that we as men can perceive. He is "not given" and as such he is the ultimate reality, the underlying ground of all existence, that which makes existence actual. So overwhelmed is Barth by this transhuman reality that he can hardly find words to "describe" it. He uses the term "indissoluble subject," which con-

fronts us as a "Thou." He thinks of God as an "Other"
whom we cannot penetrate unless he comes to us,
discloses himself to us, makes himself known to us.
As we know what we ourselves are only by meeting
others, we know ourselves fully only as we meet, or
are met by, this supreme "other," whom we call God.
The Apostles, he believes, gave witness of this God
when they preached his revelation in Jesus Christ,
and the ancient church, he is persuaded, gave expression to this belief in its dogma of the Trinity. Barth,
therefore, throws himself with all the intellectual passion that he can command into these old doctrines of
the Church, desiring to think them through from the
point of view of the revelation of God. He does not,
however, do his task well. He acts altogether too often
in a way which hides his real interest. The impression
which every unprejudiced reader must derive from his
discussion on revelation, is that a clever and exceedingly eloquent theologian has applied himself to the
old forms of theological thought with a profound emotional intellectualism, trying almost beyond the power
of his capacity to understand them. As if it were really
a matter of life and death, that as members of the
church of the Twentieth Century—we should accept
the dogma of the Trinity! Professional theologians
may think that it is absolutely necessary for us to be
concerned with the theological thought-forms of the
past, but—God be thanked!—the common Christian
layman is no professional theologian, and he may be
a better Christian just for that reason. Nor need the
preacher be a man who has developed his intellectual
theological acumen to such a degree that he can think
in the terms of the ecclesiastical philosopher of days
gone by. What he needs to know is who God is and

how man can be put in relation with him and how the relationship with God will lead him into the abundant, full, rich, meaningful life. It is only too clear that Barth, who addresses himself in his *Dogmatics* to preachers, or those who plan to be preachers intends nothing else than this. He falls short, however, in fulfilling this noble intention. He writes as an academic theologian who thinks that he must make the tradition of the church his own, and, therefore, uses all his mental powers to come close to it. Although he may imagine himself to have brought it to life again, he has rendered no real service to others who find it unnecessary to perform intellectual acrobatics for the sole purpose of understanding what people, long since dead and gone to their reward, thought and what they meant by their thoughts. Barth obscures his own plan. He wants to explain in his *Dogmatics* what makes Christian preaching Christian, and how one *can* preach and hear the Christian sermon, what it means to have a God, to be related to him and his revelation in a Christian way; but, instead of keeping this end in mind, he permits himself to fall into the error of theological hair-splitting. He forgets the truth of a saying of Harry Emerson Fosdick which he himself quotes in a recent article:[9] "Theology, like a telescope, is made simply to help people to see, and like a telescope, it is meant to be looked through and not to be looked at."

Barth's *Dogmatics* does not help people to see; it is such a complicated, highly modern and yet in many ways very antique, instrument that one is simply *forced* to look at it rather than through it.

What one is *supposed* to see is this: The good life is never identical with the *status quo*. It lies beyond

what we now are, think or do. It is released by one's
devotion to his neighbor, as he finds him in life. It is
put into action by our willingness to hear the appeal
of the other man and to follow and fulfill it. It begins
whenever we are willing to get out of our own light,
so that the other person may come into view, enter
our existence, and transform us, by liberating us from
our egohood. Christian living in particular unfolds
itself in constant self-criticism in the face of the supremely "Other," the absolute, ultimate ground of
existence, in the face of the eternal, of perfection—
of God, who is that which makes all reality real and
all spiritual truth true. It is devotion to God in such
a way that he, the absolute, perfect, eternal one, is
permitted to take possession of us, but never in the
sense that we might claim to possess him. Hence he is
always before us, never in us. Therefore, he is in every
present, unknown, yet not unknowable, unattained
yet not unattainable. In every new act of repentance,
of change of mind, of liberation from self, we are
thrown anew into his presence; but only when the last
day comes, the last day of the world, when all will
have learned to love one another, when none will live
for themselves, but all for one another, shall we see
him face to face. At the end of the world, all will be
brought under his rule. And only then shall we know
fully what perfection is, who God is. Only then shall
we enter the Kingdom of God. Until then it is our
duty, day by day, to make room for him, and in every
single act to live in the service of one another, prepar-
ing the way of the Lord, building the Kingdom of
God on earth—as far as that may be done. To this end,
in the name of that liberty which we, as the faithful,
have tasted at those moments when we ceased to think

of our macrocosmic or microcosmic selves as divine,
when we made room for God to speak and to rule
over us, God the Totally Other, the supreme ruler
over all life, we are to devote ourselves to every cause
of freedom.

.   The old Christian theology described this life,
rooted in justification, as a life of grace. Barth calls it
existence in obedience to the Word of God. "Real hearing, a hearing that really brings the existence of another than ourselves to our consciousness, a hearing
that gives us a real 'opposite,' can only be the hearing
of the word of God. In every other hearing we perceive only the echo of our own voice, and that in infinite solitariness. But the word of God erects an *authority* opposite us. That is the *nova lux et flamma,* of
which Luther once spoke. This limitation which befalls us when we hear the word of God in faith is at
once not relative but absolute, not absolute but concrete. It is absolute in so far as it ties us to God, and it
is concrete in so far as it ties us to our neighbor; it is
the real bond between our love of God and our love
of our neighbor. From this point of view the demand,
by which the holy God lays claim upon us, must be
understood as a demand for our *sacrifice* and our *service.* To God we are enthralled and to our neighbor we
are bound—by sanctification. . . ." [10]

This is what the telescope of Barth's *Dogmatics*
should help us to see; but, alas, the instrument is so
large, so complicated, so bewildering, that we actually
never come to the point of seeing. We are only given
an opportunity to notice the direction in which we
must look if we want to get a vision of the good life.
The chief weakness of Barth's theology is that it does

not present a theological anthropology; it merely gives a promise of it.

Its merit is that it brings it out clearly that in Christianity God must always be subject, the opposite, that he must take possession of us, that we can never think of possessing him. The *Dogmatics* is exclusively dedicated to the end of protecting this truth. Its *one* theme is: God speaks, man hears; and its *one* objective is directed against those who say that God is within and not opposite us. It takes a stand against those who feel that when they infinitely enlarge themselves they have found God. God is neither a small nor a large self within the human heart and within human "experience." He is the supremely other, and as such not object, but subject. We come into contact with him not by *Erlebnis, innere Erfahrung*, but by *Widerfahrnis*.

The doctrine of the Trinity, understood as the movement of God within himself, serves Barth in maintaining this idea of the subjectivity of God. The eternal Lord, whose being infolds itself in three modes of being (*Seinsweisen*) (thus Barth interprets the ancient term "person") namely as Father and Creator, Son and Reconciler, Spirit and Redeemer, moves and remains entirely within himself. His otherness is not limited in the slightest degree by his revelation in Jesus Christ nor by his descent into the heart of the believer in the form of the Holy Spirit. He moves in an inner-trinitarian, inner-divine circle even when he discloses himself to man. His inexplicable subjectivity by which "he is exclusively in himself and recognizable exclusively by himself in the *actus purissimus* of his three-fold being" [11] is thus asserted definitely.

But this is an intolerable and provoking speculation. The air of significance with which Barth presents it

cannot compel any one to consider it important.
Barth's neglect to develop a theological anthropology,
his refusal to use the insight into the character of
human life with which he originally began his prophetic onrush upon contemporary theology and religion, his failure to relate God to the actual needs and
conditions of human life now return upon him for
their revenge. He appears in the light of one who has
taken the place of the Almighty and who can speak, in
his stead, unfolding the inner secrets of his transcendent life. He himself once referred to the saying of
Luther that a God who is known *via speculationis* is
no true helper, because he is the creation of man's con-
ceited reason. How can he save himself from a similar
charge?

Can he say that he depends with Luther upon the
God who has revealed himself in Jesus Christ and has
therein made himself accessible to man? He deals so
extensively with the fact, *"Deus dixit,"* that one can
almost admit the validity of such a defense. Barth's
picture of Jesus Christ is by no means clear. The sayings which the authors of the gospel attribute to their
master are of no significance to him. The description
of Jesus's way of living with people which is so fully
given in the same reports, does not interest him. And
yet he could cite many a word of Jesus as a good
motto for his own real intention: is not Barth's whole
work but a commentary on Jesus's exclamation: "If
any man will come after me, let him deny himself,
and take up his cross daily, and follow me. For whosoever will save his life shall lose it; but whosoever
will lose his life for my sake, the same shall save it"
(Luc. IX, 23)? And is not the burden of Barth's theology summed up in the words, "No man, having put

his hand to the plough and looking back, is fit for the Kingdom of God" (Luc. IX, 62)? The teaching and the life of Jesus are entirely overlooked. Only the early Christian theology of his death and resurrection are deemed important enough to be considered as the authoritative testimony of the Apostles regarding him. The historical question as to why this theology was developed is doubtless a legitimate and even important one, but Barth does not ask it in reference to Jesus' relationship with his disciples, but only in connection with their concept of God, this being interpreted in terms of his holy transcendence, in the face of which the life of man is doomed by the radical crisis of negation and judgment. The early Christian philosophy of the atonement is occasionally suggested, but never fully developed. Mention is made of the "sacrifice" of Jesus, which constitutes the new covenant between man and God, but the religious philosophy which underlies this ancient philosophy is disregarded. Jesus is called the Reconciler, because he is looked upon as the victorious appearance of the transcendent Lord in the midst of man's contradictions toward God and toward himself; but nowhere is the character of this victory described. The idea implied in all this is that God, who is the synthesis of our conflicts and contrasts, has revealed himself as he really is; but at the decisive moment this really positive conception of God is not developed.

It is much more significant to Barth to retain even in his Christology, his emphasis upon the otherness of God, with the result that Jesus Christ is occasionally depicted as the revealer of God's inaccessibility. What else is this but pure nonsense? The logic and persistency with which this goal is pursued are truly amazing. When, in this connection, we use the word "logic" we do so consciously, for in the development of his Christology, Barth performs the astonishing trick of setting forth in a purely logical argument the reasons for the incarnation of God in Jesus Christ.

He himself points out that the doctrine of the Trinity as he conceives it can mean only that God remains fully within himself, *i.e.*, that even in the "persons" of Son and Spirit he continues to be *Deus absconditus,* God in his mysterious otherness. But how is it then possible to speak of the divine revelation? How can this majestic transcendent God become God for us? The only possibility of which Barth can think is that God becomes man as a Thou in the form of another person who addresses and speaks to us. Only as the God-man he can disclose himself to us. He must enter the sphere of human history, the realm of limitations. Man cannot meet God, man can only meet man. If God wants to meet man, he must, therefore, become man, but in such a manner that he never ceases to be the divinely Other.

Barth himself suggests that this reasoning might be suggested as of logical construction. But in self-defense he points out that he is not engaged in a *constructio a priori,* on the basis of certain logical premises, but rather in a *constructio a posteriori.* He points out also that the appearance of the God-man in the realm of history is a *fact,* and that his entire explanation depends upon its acknowledgment.

We, however, who have become not a little critical of this theology, and are full of fear lest something has been imposed upon us that we cannot accept with sincerity of heart or mind, must ask how it is possible to make this construction *a posteriori.* A fact is either recognized or it is not. No construction will make it a better or a worse one. Nor does it make any difference whether a fact is thinkable or not. If it is a fact, it must be thinkable.

Consequently, if the appearance of the God-man is a fact, it must be recognized as such. But, in this case ordinarily reliable common sense is of no use. Only if, in this regard, we are willing to declare our reasoning capacity to be out of order, can we accept the fact of the God-man as a miracle. Such an attitude requires that we presuppose the existence of supernatural powers, and the emergence of such an extraordinary human being as the God-man is then due to the act of a super-natural God, "with whom nothing is impossible."

Does Barth really mean it so? Occasionally he does indeed make use of this philosophy. We may even go so far as to say that only on this basis can he possibly develop the major part of his Christology. For what else was the presupposition of the ancient fathers who issued the decree of the Council of Chalcedon, proclaiming the dogma of the two natures of Christ, of his full divinity and full humanity? Barth repeats this dogma seriously. He finally even declares that the Virgin Birth is a necessary part of the creed of the Christian church.

Yet he does not expect us to think in the way which we have just characterized. We are not supposed to consider the appearance of the God-man and his birth of the Virgin Mary historical *facts*. We are told that the actual revelation of the majestic, inaccessible God is a super-historical (*urgeschichtlich*) event. That is to say: It is historically unknowable; it comes within the compass only of "theological knowledge." [12] For what occurs in this special event is not only history but "more-than-history," and this "more" is due to the fact that it contains the *meaning* of all history, for "its content is the Logos, from whom all that is created originally sprang, and who alone gives significance to all happenings within the created world." [18] "History is not itself super-history (*Urgeschichte*), which would be redemption, suspension of time by eternity; but it recognizes its idea (*Urbild*) or meaning as it is fulfilled in super-history. . . . Not every time is a time of revelation, but revelation may be disclosed at any time. All times may become times of prophecy, contemporaneous, simultaneous with the revelation. For they do not become contemporaneous with it in its historical effects or by means of historical tradition or by the medium of historical continuity. Super-history has no historical continuity. It is history, but it is effective as the word (speech) of God to the men both of the closest and of the most distant times. . . . That revelation is more than eternal history is evident in that it is a point in history in time. That it is more than history in time is evident in that it is not dependent upon the incontrovertible succession of history in time: all history, even history before and history after, unites itself in a circle around it as the centre. The positive revelation of all history is related to super-history as the periphery to the centre, as prophecy to fulfilment, as Advent to Christmas. Without being itself revelation any history which is connected with revelation may give testimony of it, participate in it and thus be qualified history of the second grade, history which happens because of super-history; and in so far as it is a testimony, reflex, echo of this, it is more than history. If one should wish to

give a name to this prophetic history which is thus
gathered around revelation, it will be clearest and
simplest to say that it is the *church*, the history of
God on earth, a history dominating all other history,
once for all founded in Jesus Christ." [14]

Barth warns us, in our understanding of what he
calls "*Urgeschichte*"—which we can but translate
Super-history, as being preferable to *Pre-history*—not
to think of it as something which in addition to the
quality of historicity possesses also the distinction of
being God's word. It is not interpreted history, but
an event which "in its subject is God's word and only
in its predicate an historical occurrence." [15] It is, therefore, in no way protected from being assigned to the
realm of myth. "Both superstition and real faith evidently create the myth, the unhistorical, the event
which has really taken place only in imagination." [16]
But the difference between the two is that the myth
of superstition or heresy must be considered as "non-
fact," while the myth of faith is divine fact, forever
becoming such afresh *in the act of recognition. In the
acceptance* of this super-historical event its factual
character is continued, and only in such a way does
it become truth, thus being distinguished from the
non-truth of imagination. Barth does not seem to
realize that such an attitude destroys belief in the contingency of the fact of revelation, which he otherwise
desires to maintain. The result is that he proposes a
conception of revelation-history which is plainly and
indissolubly paradoxical, affirming both the singularity and the eternity of the event.

It cannot be denied that these expositions have
much more meaning than the reconstruction of the
ancient dogma. The concept of "*Urgeschichte*," bor-

rowed from Overbeck, assumes in the hands of Barth an almost Platonic significance. It is the center of all history because, in it, meaning is realized, supreme value is fact, truth-reality is achieved, perfection is made concrete, eternity has become time, God has become man. It represents the synthesis of the contrasts within human life. As believers, we can live under its shadow, beginning new lives with it and moving toward it in anticipation of our return into it. It is true that this prehistorical, super-historical event is not in the reach of historical experience. It *is* more than that.

Is that the reason why Barth shrinks away from the "historical Jesus"? Is he afraid that historical relativism might affect the truth which stands eternally? Perhaps so. But why should Jesus not be understood as the outstanding servant of the "true myth" fulfilled? Why must the church be founded upon a Christology which is cluttered with elements of supernaturalistic superstition?—particularly since, according to Barth, not only the prophets of the Old Testament and not only the Apostles of the New Testament but also those outside of the Bible who are ambassadors of the truth that human life is under the promise of God's fulfillment, are witnesses to the one revelation.

Who would doubt that this profound philosophy is the *meaning* of the traditional systems of Christian theology? But is that sufficient reason to revive them with all their inadequate and often unintelligible terminology? Is it wholly impossible that the church as the fellowship of believers in the victory of eternity over time, in the *reality* of truth should create a new creed? In one of his addresses Barth himself deals with this problem, and points out that we stand between the times and are not yet victorious beyond the crisis. Only after that, he declares, would it be possible to formulate a new confession. What would then happen? He says: "The Bible would be read again as Holy Scripture. It would no longer be investigated for its religious, but for its objective content. Theological professors and students and the pastors at their conferences would speak again of Trinity and Predestination, of Christology, and the sacraments, and other decent things. . . . . " To this we reply that attention to the "objective content," the inner core of the Bible, the "Word" in the words, is indeed a rigid requirement for the reorientation of the church, but we deny that it is necessary that, in our efforts for a new expression of the Christian faith, we occupy ourselves with the Trinity and Christology. We would then commit the same mistake that Barth makes in his *Dogmatics*. We would become involved in theological arguments which have only historical value and which, if revived and accepted, would cause more confusion than clarification. Attention to the reality of God and not to religious experience and belief and consciousness in their several manifestations is certainly an absolute prerequisite for the rejuvenation of the church. Devotion, yes, obedience to the "Yonder," the "Not-Yet," to the "Kingdom of God which is to *come*," instead of dependence upon some inner possession which we can call our own, upon a psychological or sociological *status quo*, is our duty. But when we speak of this we must do so in the language of our own day, in the thoughts of the man of the Twentieth Century. We must be released from the duty of using the speech-forms and world-views of our fathers if we are to consecrate ourselves to the same cause as they. Supernaturalistic metaphysics are offensive to our minds and consciences; they must, therefore, be left to the mercy of historians. The superhistorical fact that God can be known only by revelation must be stated with a new mythology. The ancient church expressed it in the form of the cosmological drama with the God-man as its centre. The Reformation explained it in the form of the psychology of justification. And we . . . . . ?

First of all, we must learn again to appreciate religion as devotion to what underlies all existence, constituting it in its actual reality and in its meaning. We call this "order" God—and would that all of us could be constantly aware of the fact that "God" is primarily a word, perhaps the most significant word of our language, but nevertheless a word with a certain meaning-content! We must admit that "He" is transcendent, which means that he is not a part of us, our reason, our experience, but that we are a part of him. We therefore denominate the knowledge that we obtain of him by the word revelation (disclosure), indicating thereby that we cannot give it to ourselves, but that it must be given to us. Hence the true meaning of our lives is not one which we, out of our own wider or narrower inclinations, can put into ourselves, but which overcomes us when we feel that we belong to "God." In consequence, revelation causes an ever renewed disturbance of our self-sufficiency. It compels us to look away from our own dear selves and teaches us a sense of objectivity. It makes us view life *sub specie mortis* and *sub specie aeternitatis*. Our existence is thus gradually transformed into a devotion to God which we can realize concretely and daily by giving our attention and service to our neighbor, whoever and wherever he is, since he is a part, if not a parable, of the supreme God, who, though he transcends us, is not far from each one of us: in him we live and move and have our being. Particularly as Christians, we must realize that this attitude toward life is recommended to us by Jesus of Nazareth, who was the unequaled teacher and practicer of this faith. His death on the cross, together with the generations of Christians who have gone before us, reminds us that the truth by which we may live is acquired by and expresses itself in self-sacrifice.

If we desire to make this faith our own, we must become critics of ourselves and of our era in the name of the "new heaven and the new earth," of the world to come, when "God" will be king. We must attack all self-sufficiency in personal and social life, in marriage, in politics, economics, art and philosophy, and particularly in religion, church and theology. Man, the measure of all things—this is idolatry, against which we must arise in the name of God, who is "in heaven" and whose kingdom shall come on earth.

If Barth is a leader in the fight against this kind of idolatry, especially as it has appeared in the life of the churches, we must follow him with a will. And if the battle is won, we shall proceed to formulate a new theology—not different in content from the old, not violating the virtue and necessity of historical continuity, not new in its meaning, but contemporary in form and thought-expression, in full awareness of the wider knowledge of the life in this universe which we have gained primarily through and from that uprising against the medieval form of self-sufficiency, which we call the Reformation. In the spirit of Protestantism, we must now protest against the secularism and autonomy of modern man, its own child. No return

to the past will be of help to us. A repristination of
what has been can only mislead us.

In so far as Barth makes the attempt of a restoration
of this latter kind, he speaks to deaf ears. And it is because he really seems to move in this direction that his
prophetic voice is muffled. We need a thoroughly contemporary leader.

Barth's limitations are two-fold. He speaks too
bluntly in supernaturalistic terms. In his desire to affirm as strongly as possible the objective reality of the
God who confronts us, he is led to describe God in terms
of strictest Personism. There can be no doubt that in
such a way the otherness of the divine can best be maintained (and in a purely speculative manner it can be
assumed that the ultimate reality upon which we, together with the entire universe, depend must certainly
be no less but more than what we call personality and
must therefore include it), but it ought also to be
brought out that thus to characterize God is primarily
due to our need of speaking of him symbolically and in
the insufficient way of human language. Again and
again—perhaps in memory of his early article on the
personality of God—Barth qualifies the almost too direct emphasis upon the personal, active nature of God
by stressing his sublimity; but in his later books, he appears unduly to accentuate the *personal* sovereignty
and rulership of the eternal one. He may thereby be
in a position to bring out more fully his fundamental
conviction that faith have an "opposite." He may
thereby also be best protected against the charge
of being affected by a religious scepticism which would
forbid him to defend the idea of the reality of God—
an idea which is, indeed, of primary interest to him.
He may have been led into this particular thought-

world by the fact that he early accustomed himself
to define the relationship between God and man in
terms like "speech," "word," *etc.* The prominence of
the *"Deus dixit"* in his *Dogmatics* is almost bewildering. But to take this and similar expressions too literally
may lead to rather uncomfortable consequences; and
Barth, it seems, has not avoided one of them, when he
employs too gross a supernatural Personism.

The other limitation of his thought is closely connected with this: it is his staunch Biblicism. The Bible
is the medium through which God speaks in the words
of the prophets and apostles to the men of all times.
His revelation does not take place without the means
of their testimony. The Bible is, therefore, God's word
—not plainly, directly, but brokenly. In the human,
fallible, insufficient words of the men of the Bible the
voice of God is to be heard, for their relationship to
God's revelation was an immediate one. "The super-
historical revelation was addressed to them, and only
through them to us. . . . We believe and know because
of their testimony. . . . . A special, eminent place over
others must not be allotted to these men, neither in respect to their religion or their morality or their knowledge. A person is not a prophet or an apostle because
he is a wise man or a genius or a classic figure, but because he is a servant who performs the absolutely singular and unrepeatable office of a witness of revelation. . .
It is true that the success of the testimony of the
prophets and the apostles consists just in the fact, that
the revelation becomes real to other people in the same
way as to them, and that one can find among these
other people some to whom one cannot deny the title
of witness of Jesus Christ in a derived sense. Perhaps,
from a historical point of view, they are much more

powerful, impressive and efficient witnesses of Jesus
Christ than the men of the Bible. Why should a person
not be justified in claiming to have received more from
his devout mother than from the entire Bible? . . . .
But that is not the point in question. The Bible must
become for everyone the direct and strongest source of
his Christian *stimulation*. Many, perhaps most men,
would not be able sincerely to pretend that this was so
in their case. One might perhaps receive more from
more directly accessible witnesses and . . . still be fully
alive to the fact that besides the incidental, direct stim-
ulators, there are first-hand witnesses, by whose testimony the trustworthiness and authority of that of
our friends must be measured and proved. The pri-
ority of the word of the prophets and apostles over
other words is founded in the law of the church, and
not in any one particularly enlightening experience." [17]

But, we ask, on which grounds does the church accept the words of the men of the Bible as authoritative? Barth himself admits that as "pious confessions,
ideas, intuitions of ancient religious men" they would
not suffice for such legitimation. But he declares: "If
the church believes it has *heard* God in the testimonies
of these persons, it must also believe that God has
spoken in them. To be sure, men have spoken . . . , but
in the echo of their voices which we hear, God himself
speaks. This alone is the foundation of the respect that
the church bestows upon these witnesses. . . . " [18] The
Bible is Holy Scripture as a medium of God's voice.

Such a statement can not, of course, be proved by
historical investigation. It is part, according to Barth,
of the knowledge given by faith. But faith is not a human attitude, the result of a human value-judgment;
it is a gift of grace and as such a work of the Holy Spirit,

of God himself. When faith, therefore, recognizes the
Bible as the word of God, it participates in God's
knowledge of himself. "Wherever knowledge of God
really takes place, of God who has never been seen by
any one, it occurs by incomprehensible participation
in the knowledge which God has of himself. To speak
of God can only have the meaning of letting God himself speak." [19] This is indeed a most provoking doctrine.
Before we form an opinion about it, we should listen
still more attentively to Barth's exposition. In another
connection, he declares that the Bible is God's word
not on the basis of a judgment that we pass ourselves or
take over from others, but because of the subjection of
our own and all men's judgment to the fact, which
is exempt from all human judgment, that God speaks.
"This is a conviction which needs no proof, a knowledge which has its ratio in itself, an experience which
derives from revelation and from nowhere else... The
Bible is *known* as God's word because it *is* God's word.
If one tries another proof, one will prove something
else... It is a circle into which one cannot come from
without and out of which one cannot go from within.
One can only be either within or without. There is no
neutral position, in which one might think over the
possibilities of being within or without and arrive at
the appropriate conclusion." [20]

This presentation is a conscious repetition of the
old Calvinist doctrine of the *testimonium spiritus
sancti internum*. God, the Holy Spirit, speaks in the
words of the prophets and apostles; and God, the Holy
Spirit, hears them within us. Barth is interested in this
doctrine because he believes that it protects the Christian church from the errors of the dogma of the literal
inspiration of the Bible and of the theology of inner

experience. The Bible is not a divine oracle, true and authoritative in itself. The revelation is not an objective fact; it occurs only if it is related to one who believes it. Nor can revelation be a subjective experience in the depth of the soul. For where is the proof that it leads to God and not to a demon or even to a special sphere of the inner life? An inner experience of God is possible only if God himself is its opposite. "The Holy Spirit is neither a holy historical, nor a holy psychological doctrine, but he is God himself, acting in one single synchronous act by revelation to the prophets and apostles and by their testimony to us. . . . God speaks there and God hears here: the Bible is therefore God's word and the true church of all times hears God's word in it." [21]

After weighing these sentences, we find it difficult to understand how the word of God in the Bible is to be distinguished from the original word of God in Jesus Christ. It is a seemingly clear thought that the word of God is threefold,—in the sermon in so far as it relies upon the Scripture, and in the Scripture in so far as it gives testimony of God's immediate, superhistorical revelation in Jesus Christ. But when one remembers that Barth's chief concern is to point out that God is the subject of the revelation and that he is to be understood as the living God, one encounters almost unthinkable barriers.

Barth recommends the following theology: God is one; he is indissoluble subject; he is the totally other Thou that confronts us; in him alone we can truly exist. Therefore we, who are now living, struggling for our true existence, must seek him and nothing else. We are told to believe that he has condescended to come to us, that he has entered our world, our own individual world, and that he has redeemed us. In that mode of his being which is called spirit, he has entered our hearts. This spirit has come to us in the sermon, in the human words of one who speaks in the name of God. The preacher can communicate God only because God himself speaks in him, a fallible, unholy, undivine person. The Holy Spirit hears in us and speaks in him. But this is possible only because he who addresses us in the name of God out of the Holy Spirit has received it through the not infallible medium of the historical church (which believes by the grace of the same spirit) from the prophets and apostles of the Bible. These men, thoroughly human just as we, by grace of the same spirit, had become witnesses to God's revelation which had taken place in Jesus Christ— whom those who can believe by the mercy of God the Spirit recognize as God in the second mode of his existence, the Son, in whom God has become incarnate. Jesus Christ, the Son, reveals God in the first mode of his existence, as the Father and Creator. That God, Father, Son, and Holy Spirit are one, this *mysterium trinitatis*, is the secret of God alone. As the triune God, he confronts us in our existence. It has pleased him to reveal himself to us, not directly, but indirectly: he who lives in a light no man can approach unto, discloses himself to us only in concealment—in Jesus Christ and him crucified, through the unliterary words of the unbeautiful and unexcellent men of the Bible, and through the often untrue, altogether too human words of the preachers of the church. We certainly cannot command him. Even if out of our own decision or willingness or sincere desire we should long to have him come to us, we cannot find him, except the Holy Spirit should lighten the darkness of our hearts, predestining us thereby to salvation, which is in God and from God alone. Thus, mystery of mysteries, God the Spirit speaks and God the Spirit hears, and fortunate, indeed, is he, in whom God, out of his infinite mercy and wisdom makes his habitation!

Why God does not reveal himself directly but only through the mediacy of his witnesses—this too is hidden in his own counsel.

It must be plain that such a theology is conceivable only with the presupposition of a belief in a being— yes, we must say; supernatural *person* who, in miraculous, by many uncontrollable ways, governs our lives according to his arbitrary decision. It is astonishing that Barth can say so much about God. But of course, we must not forget that our analysis of his ideas is based only upon the first volume of his *Dogmatics*. The strictly dogmatic chapters are not yet published. It would certainly not be unlogical, if Barth should there revive the conceptions of God and the theological notions of the generations of the past together with their whole milieu of superstitious and weird thoughts about the world and life.

Why, we ask ourselves in utter amazement, was it necessary for Barth to renew the structure of the theological thought of the past as he has? Was there no other way of developing a theocentric theology? Does the church make such a demand? Barth would probably answer in the affirmative. So often he refers to the authority of the church. That he is primarily concerned for its welfare, no one can doubt who has read his most recent articles, which are almost entirely devoted to theological church politics. Nor can one forget that he began his career as a "theologian" in the active ministry.

But the church in whose name he speaks is the church
of the past. In consequence he is not in the position to
speak the saving word for the present. He is absolutely convinced of the fact that during the last two
hundred years, but particularly since Schleiermacher,
Protestant Christianity has betrayed its cause, because
it has lost the "Realism of God," the belief in the reality
of God. In our analysis of Barth's writings, we have attempted to show that the recovery of this lost treasure
is a necessity. In so far as he argues on the basis of the
problem of the meaning of life, we have been able to
follow him. But this existential method is only partly
followed in his dogmatic discussions. The method
which he really follows is characterized by the acceptance of ecclesiastical tradition and of Biblical authority.
Thereby he evinces a definite sympathy for the view-
points of Roman Catholicism and orthodox Protestantism. Although he does not hesitate, in harmony with
critical theology, to admit the validity of a historical
analysis of the Bible and the tradition of the church,
he claims that in them the absolute authority of God
himself comes to expression. *God himself* speaks in
Jesus Christ, in the words of the Bible, and in the message of the church—in so far, at least, as it accepts the
authority of the canon of the Bible. God *has* revealed
himself. Upon such a theological foundation one can
erect only the building of a new Scholasticism. Just as
the medieval scholastics rearranged the traditional
dogmas of the church according to the demands of
philosophical principles and for the purpose of proving them true, Barth reviews given theological doctrines, in his *Dogmatics* generally those of Calvinism,
under the aspect of the "crisis." If his philosophy of
life were not born in the pains of the search of the mod-

ern man for truth, for the meaning of life, one could indeed think that he had simply returned to the past. But his modern temper is too apparent. Hence he evokes our interest in spite of the almost intolerable theological skeleton-dance which he forces upon us. It *is* a *fact* that the supernatural authority of old theology is *dead*. The miracles of God's personal appearance in Jesus Christ and of the divine inspiration of the Bible are dead. No dialectics will resurrect them. Only a *sacrificium intellectus* can. And that is a crime which no one may commit without terrific punishment. *But God is not dead,* as truly as we live and as truly as we seek him. Modern theology is right when it refuses to think in terms of supernaturalistic metaphysics. It is wrong when it is satisfied with a psychological anthropology. For at the end of this road is but man in his solitariness—without God. There is no salvation in that. But man *must* be saved—from *himself*. Therefore, he needs God—opposite himself, but not outside of his life.

Barth's *Dogmatics* is significant because it gives expression to this need, because it explains what ought to be. It is an expression of the modern temper which longs for God, for the real God.

VIII

CONCLUSION

A SUMMARY of the results of our analysis of Barth's theology is superfluous. Its main tendencies have been pointed out in a sincere effort to understand them. In the course of this enterprise, we could not refrain from becoming critical. We have not concealed our sympathy and agreement, and we have not spared words of protest. Whether the judgment here passed on Barth's thinking is just, we cannot say. It must be taken as *one* opinion of a theology which may be considered the most provoking of our day.

In conclusion, we turn once more to the fundamental theme of the dialectical theology. A quotation from a lecture on "The Word of God in Theology from Schleiermacher to Ritschl" may serve as a starting-point. Barth writes: [1]

"In my understanding, the problem of the *word*— *i.e.*, the word of *God* in theology, is the question whether and in how far theology is conscious of its task of directing the Christian sermon to an expression in human words of what is said to man by God himself about God, in contrast to all that man may tell himself about God. . . . .

"At two points, it may be decided whether or not the concept of the Word governs a theology, *i.e.*

whether or not it realizes that the Christian sermon
is a repetition of what man has been told by God.
First, in its understanding of the Christian man of
the present: does he, precisely as a Christian man,
stand *opposite* to the truth of God, again and again
opposite to a truth which must really come to him?
Does he face it, every morning afresh, as one who
does not know and, therefore, only hears it, as one
who does not control it and, therefore, obeys? Is his
cognition of it really recognition? Or does he *not*
stand opposite of it, does it not need to come to him,
because he already knows or has it; because, somehow, he owns it, so that he has but to recall it; because he is master of it? In the first case, he lets God
tell him what is necessary. In the second case, he tells
himself what is necessary. Theology must choose.
That is the *psychological* aspect of the problem. But
the judgment may be made also at a second point:
in the understanding of the relationship between
God's truth and history. Does the truth of God
stand opposite to man also in history, as a reality absolutely different from him, absolutely condescend-
ing to him, so that he can in no way acquire or safeguard it for himself, and so that he can know it only
in so far as it gives itself to him, so that he knows it
only by being known in it? Is revelation history because it pleases God to disclose himself in history, and
is his divine pleasure a question which man cannot
consider answered even for a moment? Or is history
revelation, because it pleases man to study history
and to find God in it? Has man access to the truth
of God through history ... in such a way that he interprets history in the light of what is or has become
truth to him? In the first case, he lets truth be told

to him; in the second place, he tells it to himself, *via* history. Here too, theology has to choose. And this is the *historical* aspect of the problem. ....

"The theology of the first half of the Nineteenth Century instructed the Christian preacher that man is in a position to seek, find and possess the truth of God in his own Christian consciousness, or in history, so that he, the preacher, might say not what had been told to him, but what he might, could, and should tell of himself. That is what was called the word of God, at that time."

These sentences clearly describe the chief concern of Barth. He is opposed to any sort of theology which holds God to be given in inner or historical experience. He objects to modern theology in so far as it is dominated by Psychologism and Historism. God is transcendent. He is not a fact of personal experience or of history. He is a reality radically different from that which we find a *priori* or *a posteriori* in and through our consciousness. He is unknown except as he reveals himself. He is the subject and not the object of revelation. Man cannot control him but he controls man. God is God, not man.

In the background of this theology is the conviction that if man absolutizes anything that he might claim to have, he deceives himself, for his life is constantly challenged by the danger of meaninglessness. Any form of human self-sufficiency is exposed to the curse of illusoriness. It becomes especially dangerous in the field of religion. For if God—in whom the question of the meaning of life is answered, because he is that which makes all reality real and truth true, because he is reality full of truth and truth full of reality—should really be naught but an element of human life, if his being should be a possession, or a quality, or a content of human consciousness, he too would be as questionable and uncertain as the life of man. A theology, therefore, which explains the divine revelation on the basis of psychological or historical analyses is incapable of asserting the reality of God, without the certainty of which man cannot meaningfully live.

From the viewpoint of the history of modern theology, it is significant that the work of Ludwig *Feuerbach* has made a profound impression on Barth. In all his writings, he alludes to the writings of this philosopher, and in his book on *Theology and the Church*, he devotes a whole chapter [2] to him. This man is, in many ways, a forerunner of what we now call religious humanism. He considered the idea of God and all religious concepts products of the imagination of man, reflections of human desires into a transcendent realm. He asked the question whether the nature of God is anything else than the nature of man, objectified in such a manner that it appears as an "opposite" of man, and whether theology, therefore, should not frankly be regarded as anthropology. In consequence he desired to change men from "friends of God to friends of men, from believers to thinkers, from worshippers to workers, from candidates for the 'Yonder' to students of the 'Here,' from Christians, who according to their own confession are partly animals and partly angels, to men, whole men." [3] According to Barth these views constitute very legitimate questions for modern theology. He believes that from its own premises one can do no other than finally agree with Feuerbach when he asserts that modern theology is tending toward the apotheosis of man. He is of course sure that the theologians do not mean it so, but he is certain that only that can be the end of their road. It is highly interesting to note that certain American preachers have frankly professed opinions which are essentially the same as Feuerbach's.

In the mind of Barth, the underlying conviction on which this sort of thinking is based is that "man is the measure of all things and that he is the essence, origin and goal of all *values*." And "if one cannot laugh Feuerbach out of countenance when he proposes such a view, one cannot attack him critically," [4] Barth believes. Only ignorance of death and ignorance of evil can be the basis of such a philosophy. A person who knows that he must die and that he is evil will wisely refrain from identifying himself in any way with God.

Humanism is not profound enough to be credited with the name of a religious philosophy which is oriented to a knowledge of man as he really is. The fact of death must at least compel a man to ask himself the question, *why* live—and just this question the Humanists avoid. For that reason, they are liable to produce a state of mind which must be characterized as human self-sufficiency, which is not in need of the real God. Barth fears that the dependence of modern theology upon psychological and historical "experiences" and upon the beliefs resulting from them does not permit a sure defense against the humanization of God which Feuerbach and the Humanists propagate. Hence he struggles for a theology which will be based on the faith in the ultra-human, real God.

But where is this God? That he is, must simply be believed. The "existence" of the real God is an axiom, a *principium*,[5] to which one cannot ascend, but from which one can only come. We have attempted to show that this conviction is part of a religious philosophy

of life described by the word "crisis," which is the
background of Barth's entire thinking. The infinite
contradictions in the existence of man are dissolved
only in a transcending synthesis toward which he constantly moves in a life of repentance and of an ever
renewed spirit of unselfishness, criticizing himself in
the presence of the eternal perfection and in anticipation of the Kingdom of God to come.

We believe that this philosophy of life is true and
profound. In its presentation lies the strength of Barth.
It must, therefore, be regretted that he has as yet not
developed it fully.

His real interest is more concretely theological. He
understands himself as a member of the Christian
church, and wishes to be an ecclesiastical thinker.
Hence he is not satisfied with the recovery of the meaning of the religious idea of revelation as it underlies
this philosophy of life, but he strives to restore also a
definitely Christian concept of the revelation. He
thinks on the basis of the Christian belief that God has
revealed himself in Jesus Christ. It is in reference to
this specific theology that we must object to Barthianism, for it becomes finally a restoration of Christian
traditionalism. God has revealed himself in Jesus Christ
—this is the claim of the Bible and this claim must be
obediently recognized. That God has revealed himself
in Jesus Christ is the theme of the authoritative theologies of the Church universal and this theme must be
recognized. The sacrament of baptism must even serve
as a guarantee of the truth and trustworthiness of the
belief of the church. In consequence, Barth is led to renew the dogmatic theology of the past; and one cannot
avoid the accusation that he ultimately presents himself
as a devotee of a modern scholasticism. This tendency

of his thought, which grows in definiteness as the years pass, must deprive him of the privilege of leadership in the present dilemma of Christian theology. In the first place, the church which could exercise such teaching authority as Barth presupposes, does not really exist. He himself once exclaimed: "A very essential condition of the misery of contemporary theology is the fact that we theologians have no church behind us, which has the courage to tell us clearly: In so far as we have the right to speak, such and such is dogma *in concretissimo.*" [6] There is no longer such a church—except in the case of Catholicism. How can one then construct a theology which presupposes such ecclesiastical authority? And furthermore: The theory that the claim of the prophets and apostles of the Bible *must* be recognized as true, is arbitrary. Why not also the testimony of other prophets and founders of religion?

It was not without reason that modern theology has developed as it has. *The world and man's world-consciousness have changed.* The sciences, *including* the science of religion, are young. We *must* acknowledge that the authorities lodged in Bible and Church were supernatural! And they have fallen under the assault of a tremendous increase of knowledge and criticism. The absoluteness and the truth of the Christian religion, as it is based upon the belief in God's exclusive revelation in Jesus Christ, can no longer be asserted in the old ways, not even in modernized old ways. One cannot combat the methods of modern theology, its Psychologism and Historism, by attempting a recovery of the old authorities against which it rightly and necessarily rebelled.

Barth's criticism of liberal theology, however, can hardly be refuted. The premises of that theology, in-

deed, seem hardly strong enough to defend the belief
in God against the religious agnosticism which is called
Humanism. Barth's rediscovery of the transcendence
of God and of the eschatological nature of the religious
life are expressions of a truly profound and genuine
view of life. The theologians will have to accept the
correction which is derived from the recognition of the
"Biblical attitude" and of the "infinite, qualitative difference between time and eternity." They will also
have to take the significance of the religious "crisis"
into consideration. But another than Barth will have
to come, to apply these principles to modern theology.
We cannot go back behind Troeltsch, Harnack, Ritschl
and Schleiermacher. We can go only beyond them.

Barth is not *the* prophet of the new Christianity. He
is the "preacher in the wilderness." His voice rings in
our ears, and we will not forget his message, but we
must wait for another. Perhaps this is what he would
wish us to do.

God is God, not man—repent ye! This is his admo-
nition to us. If we accept it, we must endeavor to live
in an attitude of mind the light of which shines through
all the stormy and cloudy passages of Barth's dialectics
and which Luther beautifully described in the following words: "*Dass also dies Leben nicht ist eine Frumm-
keit, sondern ein Frommwerden, nicht eine Gesund-
heit, sondern ein Gesundwerden, nicht ein Wesen,
sondern ein Werden, nicht eine Ruhe, sondern eine
Übung: wir sind's noch nicht, wir werden's aber. Es
ist noch nicht getan und gescheben, es ist aber in Gang
und Schwang. Es ist nicht das Ende, es ist aber der Weg;
es glühet und glinzt noch nicht alles, es fügt sich aber
alles.*"[7]

APPENDIX

A LIST OF BARTH'S PUBLICATIONS

Moderne Theologie und Reichgottesarbeit. Zeitschrift für Theologie und Kirche (Z. Th. K.), 1909, pp. 317-21.
Der Glaube an den persönlichen Gott. Z. Th. K., 1914, pp. 21-32; 65-95.
Der Römerbrief. First edition (R. 1). Bern: G. A. Bläschlin, 1919. Second edition (R.), München: Kaiser, 1922. Fifth ed., 1926.
Das Wort Gottes und die Theologie. (W. G.), Gesammelte Vorträge, Vol. I. München: Kaiser, 1922; second ed. 1925. Engl. translation by Douglas Horton: *The Word of God and the Word of Man.* Boston: Pilgrim Press, 1928.
Die Auferstehung der Toten (A.). München: Kaiser, 1924; second ed. 1926.
Die Christliche Dogmatik im Entwurf. Vol. I: *Die Lehre vom Worte Gottes.* Prolegomena zur christlichen Dogmatik. München: Kaiser, 1927.
Erklärung des Philipperbriefes. München: Kaiser, 1928.
Die Theologie und die Kirche. Gesammelte Vorträge, Vol. II. (Th. K.). München: Kaiser, 1928.
Vom Christlichen Leben. München: Kaiser, 1923. Engl. translation by J. Strathearn McNab: *The Christian Life.* London: Student Christian Movement Press, 1930.
Zur Lehre vom Heiligen Geist. München: Kaiser, 1930.

There are two collections of sermons by K. Barth and E. Thurneysen: *Komm Schöpfer Geist* (second ed., München: Kaiser, 1924) and *Suchet Gott, so werdet Ihr leben* (second ed., 1928).

Barth is a regular contributor to the journal *Zwischen den Zeiten* (Z. Z.), edited by *Georg Merz* in München (Kaiser). His most recent articles have appeared in this *Zeitschrift.*

Chapter I: [1] Visser 't Hoofts, *The Background of the Social Gospel in America.* Haarlem (Holland): H. D. Tjeenk Willink, 1928.
[2] Fritz Heinemann, *Neue Wege der Philosophie.* Leipzig: Quelle und Meyer, 1929. Friedrich Karl Schumann, *Der Gottesgedanke und der Zerfall der Moderne.* Tübingen: Mohr, 1929. Paul Tillich, *Die religiöse Lage der Gegenwart.* Berlin: Ullstein, 1926. Wilhelm Koepp, *Die gegenwärtige Geisteslage und die dialektische Theologie.* Tübingen: Mohr, 1930.

Chapter II: [1] See the article on "Offenbarung," by Paul Tillich, in the theological encyclopædia *Religion in Geschichte und Gegenwart* (second ed. Tübingen: Mohr, 1927 ff.)
[2] For a major part of the discussion of this chapter I am indebted to Werner Wiesner, *Das Offenbarungsproblem in der dialektischen Theologie.* München: Kaiser, 1930.
[3] Friedrich Schleiermacher, *The Christian Faith.* English translation from the second German edition (1830), ed. by H. R. Mackintosh and J. S. Stewart. Edinburgh: T. and T. Clark, 1928, p. 14.
[4] *Ibid.,* p. 14. [5] *Ibid.,* p. 50. [6] *Ibid.,* p. 385. [7] *Ibid.,* p. 63.
[8] See Ferdinand Kattenbusch, *Die deutsche evangelische Theologie seit Schleiermacher.* Fifth ed. Giessen: Töpelmann, 1926, p. 102.

Chapter III: [1] Th. K. pp. 240 ff. [2] Z. Th. K. 1909, pp. 317-321. [3] *Ibid.,* pp. 479-488. [4] Z. Th. K. 1914, pp.21-32, 65-95. [5] W. G. p. 22. [6] W. G. p. 24. [7] G. A. Bläschlin, Bern. [8] See the review by Professor Ph. Bachmann in *Neue Kirchliche Zeitschrift,*

FOOTNOTE REFERENCES 223

1921, p. 533. [9]R. 1, p. 153. [10]W. G., p. 100 ff. [11]W. G., pp. 45, 64 ff. [12]Z. Z., 1927, pp. 514-515.

Chapter IV: [1]R., pp. IX ff. [2]R., p. XII. [3]A., p. 112. [4]Z. Z., 1926, p. 100. [5]W. G., p. 186. [6]W. G., pp. 188 f. [7]W. G., pp. 199 ff. [8]W. G., pp. 206 ff.

Chapter V: [1]R., p. 292. [2]R., p. 193. [3]D., p. 68 ff. [4]R., p. 424. [5]R. Strauch, *Die Theologie Karl Barths.* Second ed., München: Kaiser, 1925, p. 12. [6]E. Brunner, *The Theology of Crisis.* New York: Scribner's, 1930, p. 28 n. [7]R., p. 243. [8]R., p. 241. [9]R., pp. 74, 217, 183. [10]R., p. 184. [11]R., p. 73. [12]W. G., p. 77 ff. [13]W. G., p. 80. [14]R., p. 261 f. [15]R., pp. 398, 373. [16]R., p. 64. [17]R., p. 76. [18]Strauch, p. 34. [19]R., p. 412 ff. [20]R., pp. 304, 449, 479.

Chapter VI: [1]D., p. 1. [2]D., pp. 19 ff. [3]D., p. 41. [4]D., p. 47. [5]D., p. 54. [6]D., p. 56. [7]D., p. 63. [8]D., p. 69 f. [9]D., p. 70. [10]D., p. 84. [11]D., p. 87. [12]D., pp. 89 f. [13]D., p. 95. [14]D., p. 106. [15]Z. Z., 1929, pp. 309-348.

Chapter VII: [1]D., p. 127. [2]D., p. 169. [3]D., p. 134 ff. [4]D., p. 171 ff. [5]D., p. 80 f. [6]D., p. 175 ff. [7]D., p. 188 f. [8]D., p. 204 ff. [9]Z. Z., 1930, p. 384. [10]*Heiliger Geist,* p. 83 f. [11]Th. K., p. 264. [12]D., p. 264. [13]D., p. 238. [14]D., p. 238 ff. [15]D., p. 272. [16]D., p. 273. [17]D., p. 341 f. [18]D., p. 337. [19]D., p. 337. [20]D., p. 356. [21]D., p. 363.

Conclusion: [1]Th. K., p. 190 ff. [2]Th. K., p. 212 ff. [3]Quoted by Barth from Feuerbach: Th. K., p. 214. [4]Th. K., p. 237. [5]D., p. 107. [6]D., p. 307. [7]Grund und Ursach aller Artikel D. Martin Luthers so durch römische Bulle unrechtlich verdammt sind. Works (Weimar ed.), Vol. 7, p. 337. An English translation (Works of Martin Luther, ed. by H. E. Jacobs, Philadelphia: Holman, 1915 ff., Vol. III, p. 31) follows: "This life, therefore, is not righteousness but growth in righteousness, not health but healing, not being but becoming, not rest but exercise; we are not yet what we shall be, but we are growing toward it; the process is not yet finished, but it is going on; this is not the end, but it is the road; all does not yet gleam with glory, but all is being purified."

INDEX